D1572332

HOW WE GOT
THE BIBLE

HOW WE GOT THE BIBLE

Lenet Hadley Read

Deseret Book

Salt Lake City, Utah

First printing November 1985

Library of Congress Catalog Card Number 85-72842
ISBN 0-87579-799-X

Printed in the United States of America
10   9   8   7   6   5   4   3

Dedicated to my parents,
Leroy and Jennette Hadley,
and to my grandmother, Shirley,
through whom I inherited
a love of the scriptures

Contents

1 A Testament Is Established   1

2 The Word Is Preserved   13

3 A New Word Is Added to the Old   25

4 Early Christian Usage of the Scriptures   37

5 Glimmers of Light in Darkness   49

6 No Price Too Great   65

7 The Sweet and Ripened Fruit   81

8 The Power of the Word   93

9 The Gift of Latter-day Light   101

Conclusion   111

Notes   113

Genealogy of the King James Bible   124

Index   127

CHAPTER ONE

A Testament Is Established

A certain Christian man laboring in India offered to give interested natives a copy of the Bible. After hearing of its message, many eagerly responded. One old man, looking upon the Bible with reverence, asked, "How long has this book been in the world?" When he learned it had existed for centuries, he sorrowfully shook his head. "I am an old man. All my friends have died hopeless. . . . And all this time the book was here and nobody brought it to me."[1] How quickly he sensed the worth of his new possession: a record of God's dealings with man from the time of the Creation.

The Bible is indeed a book of immense consequence. Book of Mormon prophets who in visions saw it come forth testified of its great value. For Lehi, the word of God was the physical reality behind the iron rod that led unwaveringly to the tree of life. (See 1 Ne. 15:23-24.) For Nephi, the Jewish record was the "book of the Lamb of God" (1 Ne. 13:28), not fully whole nor pure, but nevertheless of great worth. Indeed, the record was so vital that Lehi was commanded to take a copy of one record as then compiled—the brass plates—with him to the promised land, in spite of jeopardy to his sons' lives and the ultimate cost of Laban's.

But we also learn from the Book of Mormon how generally

unappreciated the biblical record is. In his prophecies about the future, Nephi speaks of the lack of gratitude to the Jews for their great sacrifices in bringing forth their books: "What thank they the Jews for the Bible which they receive from them? . . . Do they remember the travails, and the labors, and the pains of the Jews, and their diligence unto me, in bringing forth salvation unto the Gentiles? . . . Have ye obtained a Bible save it were by the Jews? (2 Ne. 29:4, 6.)

Surely the sacrifices the Jews have made in bringing forth and preserving their precious records through centuries of tribulation are immense. Yet that is only a part of the drama. The whole history of the formation of the Bible, Old Testament and New, and of the efforts to preserve it and make it available in the tongues of common men are fascinating stories of special blessing by God and of utmost sacrifice by man.

In fact, the stories behind the creation of the Bible contain the best elements of storytelling: conflict, pathos, tragedy, irony, humor, awe—even intrigue. We have much to learn. But hopefully in our learning we will gain most of all a deep appreciation for the heavy cost—in self-denial and in lives—that enabled us to have these holy messages.

Precisely how and when did the "record of the Jews" begin? Most scholars say we don't know, that the stories were passed down orally, that other than oral communication began with hieroglyphics and evolved into writing. They say that the records we have of the Creation and the first patriarch came from several unknown sources at much later dates and were somehow interwoven untidily into the Genesis account.

But Latter-day Saints have a different understanding. By revealing to the Prophet Joseph Smith the writings of Moses, the Lord revealed anew to mankind when and how the record began: "A book of remembrance was kept . . . in the language of Adam, for it was given unto as many as called upon God to write by the spirit of inspiration; and by them their children were taught to read and write, having a language which was pure and undefiled. . . . This was the book of the generations of Adam, saying: In the day that God created man, in the likeness of God made he him." (Moses 6:5-6, 8.)

Thus we learn through revelation that after man's creation,

he was not left ignorant of his origins. From the beginning he was given a knowledge of writing and thereafter recorded his origins and all things that happened to him. The "record of the Jews," then, has its roots not in an accident or an afterthought, but in a gift of love from a wise and loving Creator.

In view of current scholarly opinions, these are bold assertions. Nevertheless, with new archaeological discoveries and the uncovering of more and more ancient writings, there is a growing body of evidence that the book of Moses' account of the beginning of written history is correct. Dr. Hugh Nibley has detailed the kinds of findings now uncovered. Of particular interest because it highlights the value of the ancient texts is a statement found in the writing of a pharaoh who lived long before Christ in the Thirteenth Dynasty: "My heart yearned to behold the most ancient books of Atum [Adam]. Open them before me for diligent searching, that I may know god as he really is!"[2] Early Jewish apocryphal texts also equate Adam with writing, and ancient cultures have left evidence of a belief that writing came not through man, but was a gift handed down from heaven.[3]

In addition, a leather scroll which may be the oldest book yet found has surprised scholars with its remarkably well-developed teachings of a "council in heaven, the creation of the world, the fall of man, and the means by which he may achieve resurrection and be reinstated in his primal glory."[4]

But the most important aspect of all this evidence is the excitement it should give us to recognize anew what a treasure we have. Dr. Nibley builds upon a suggestion that the semitic alphabet almost seems to have been devised for the very purpose of recording scriptures: "Whoever reads the standard works today has before him the words of God to men from the beginning, in witness of which the very letters on the page are but slightly conventionalized forms of the original symbols in which the message was conveyed. . . . As members of the human race we are bound to approach the scriptures with new feelings of reverence and respect."[5] What a difference it makes to know that the Bible did not begin in uncertain origin or with uncertain authority, but was given to man from the beginning as an essential tool to prepare him for salvation!

Latter-day revelation has also shown that the pattern of record-keeping established by Adam continued with succeeding patriarchs, who added accounts of their own days. Enoch speaks of the record of his fathers: "Death hath come upon our fathers; nevertheless we know them, and cannot deny, and even the first of all we know, even Adam. For a book of remembrance we have written among us." (Moses 6:45-46.)

Abraham testified that the process of adding to the record continued after the flood and included his own additions: "The records of the fathers, even the patriarchs, . . . the Lord my God preserved in mine own hands; therefore, a knowledge of the beginning of the creation, and also of the planets, and of the stars, as they were made known unto the fathers, have I kept even unto this day, and I shall endeavor to write some of these things upon this record, for the benefit of my posterity that shall come after me." (Abr. 1:31.)

Thus the Pearl of Great Price accounts repeatedly refer to the scriptures as a family or genealogical record going back to the Creation itself. R. K. Harrison substantiates that view. In referring to the biblical phrase "these are the generations of . . . ," he states that the Hebrew term translated "generation" means a history, narrative, or genealogical record. The phrase "These are the generations of Noah" (Gen. 6:9) could justifiably be translated, "This is the history written (or possessed) by Noah." This phrase occurs ten times in Genesis with each successive patriarch.[6]

Part of the calling of the patriarch was to make a record of his days. Thus, in relay form records from earlier patriarchs were handed down, and later prophets synthesized them, incorporated their own records, and passed them on again to yet future generations.

Although Latter-day Saint scriptures for over a hundred and fifty years have described this process, non-LDS clues are only now being found by scholars of the world. Among some of the most interesting manuscript finds of recent years are works bearing the names of ancient patriarchs. We must remember that these manuscripts are generally *not* the original writings, but they form a tradition that witnesses that original documents once existed.

These recent finds are of keen interest to Latter-day Saints because, despite their corruptions, they all contain a basic pattern that coincides with the experiences of the prophets whose records came into the hands of Joseph Smith. To summarize this pattern, each prophet separately testifies that he, deeply distressed by the sinfulness of his day, and desiring to serve God, was moved to seek the Lord earnestly. Each was subsequently given a vision in which he beheld God and portions of His glory. As part of this vision, he is taught a plan of salvation, beholds many worlds besides this one, and is shown the history of the earth. Then he is authorized and admonished to preach repentance unto his people. Sometimes there is a brief interlude between a first and second vision in which the prophet is confronted by Satan, who seeks to thwart God's work through temptation and fear.[7]

The repetitiveness of this basic pattern can add much to our understanding of the fuller record upon which the biblical account draws. The Pearl of Great Price tells us why the Bible is missing the fuller story: "Now of this thing Moses bore record; but because of wickedness [lack of belief?] it is not had among the children of men." (Moses 1:23.)

Man's scientific pursuit of the knowledge of his origins will surely lead him to some truths, but in the meantime, he is susceptible to many false conclusions. For example, discovered in ruins of Israel's neighboring cultures are stories similar to those in Genesis, such as the Creation and the Flood. Their discovery made it popular for a time to suggest that Israel had borrowed its "history" from myths of surrounding cultures. However, as time has brought new discoveries, the older, clearer, and much more believable records fall back into Israel's line.[8] Now it is more accepted among scholars that Israel's history was what gave rise to or was borrowed by others. The validity of Israel's history is shown in statements by biblical archaeologists who have found many evidences confirming the historical statements of the Bible. And some say that after years of searching they can find *no* archaeological evidence that *contradicts* the historical basis of the scriptures.[9]

From the fragments of truth that they had borrowed or inherited, other ancient cultures devised myths and legends as they separated themselves substantially from the doctrines sustaining the biblical stories. In the case of the Egyptians, their records became a grab bag full of unsorted and unclear beliefs and ideas. While their collection contained fragments of truth, those fragments were lost in a maze of confusion.

Another striking distinction separating Israel's earliest records from those of her neighbors is the hope underlying Israel's record. The prophets showed that meaning, purpose, and order control man's existence; if God did not always appear merciful to Israel, he at least operated with reasoned justice, and there was always the promise of God's prophesied redemption.

Thus while neighboring cultures had bits and pieces of truth, their records and therefore their understanding were corrupted. On the other hand, among the Hebrews fuller records of truth were meticulously kept, and the patriarchs took pains to see that the truths were passed on to other generations in as uncorrupted a form as possible. Thus, in spite of errors that have crept into them over the centuries, these records have come to us as an essential part of a true and priceless heritage.

Moses' Hand upon the Record

Although Adam and succeeding patriarchs left records, the first five books of the Old Testament are identified as the writings of Moses. How did Moses come to receive credit for these essential books?

One theory holds that such credit is misleading. A number of modern scholars point to evidence suggesting that several persons, probably none of them Moses, wrote these books. They point out that Moses' death is a part of the record and show how the books are written in differing styles and points of view.

Bruce R. McConkie categorically rejects such theories and classifies them as a product of the apostasy.[10] The Pearl of Great Price gives us revelation on this subject: "The Lord spake unto Moses, saying: Behold, I reveal unto you concerning this heaven, and this earth; *write the words which I speak.* . . . In the beginning I created the heaven." (Moses 2:1; italics added.)

We see that Moses did make a record and that he was instructed to begin with the Creation. And there is other substantiation for such a view. Apocryphal literature, the Bible itself, and both Jewish and early Christian tradition all support the belief that Moses wrote the first five books of the Bible.

But what about the changes in writing style? The continuing discovery of ancient records contradicts the theory that changes in style in the Pentateuch (Moses' five books) indicate multiple authorship. As other manuscripts of that general age and area are carefully studied, it is seen that ancient peoples commonly used a variety of styles in one composition. Some scholars now think that archaeological discoveries have rendered unsound the trend to find many unknown sources behind each book of the Bible.

Still, it is not necessary to argue that Moses' hand was the only one that touched the papyrus. Joseph Smith and other prophets used scribes to assist them, and we know that Moses understood the principle of delegation. With the major responsibilities that were his, it is possible that he assigned scribes to carry out, under his direction, part of the actual work of record-keeping, including a scribe who completed the record after Moses' death. Nibley shows that any writing of the Egyptians or Hebrews was credited to that individual who commissioned, supervised, and approved it.[11]

Furthermore, as we learn from the Book of Mormon and the Pearl of Great Price, some prophets were instructed to edit and abridge the records as they passed them along. So in addition to writing down his own revelations, Moses may have edited previous writings; and his writings may have been edited still later by others. The point remains that as long as Moses was the motivating force behind the compilation of the Pentateuch and was its principal author or reviewer, it justifiably bears his name.

The Book—Lost and Found

The law given through Moses differs from written law possessed by other ancient cultures during the same time period: instead of dealing with possessions only, Israel's law reflected the value and importance of the people. These important laws, covenants, and commandments came with a built-in warning: "These words, which I command thee this day, shall be in thine heart: and thou shalt teach them diligently unto thy children, and shalt talk of them when thou sittest in thine house, and when thou walkest by the way, and when thou liest down, and when thou risest up. . . . And they shall be as frontlets between thine eyes." (Deut. 6:6-8.)The purpose of this warning? That they might never be forgotten.

And yet, they were forgotten.

Much of Israel's story revolves around the people's failure to remember their beginnings and the messages of the Law and to adhere to its recorded covenants—even though the Law had been written and placed in the most sacred of all places, the ark of the covenant. There were a few faithful who remembered: Samuel "did let none of [God's] words fall to the ground." (1 Sam. 3:19.) But the obedience of the people generally was not nearly so great. Not only did they forget the words of the book, but they also forgot the book itself, which had been transferred to the temple along with the ark of the covenant.

The Babylonian captivity evidently cut the Israelites off even further from the book. The evidence of its loss is shown by the joy in its restoration. When the Israelites returned from captivity, among the foremost happenings associated with their freedom was the reading of the sacred words. Ezra, the scribe, was asked to read to them again what had become only dim memory. The story is very touching: the people gathered "as one man" to hear; the reading was "from morning until midday," and "the ears of all the people were attentive." They wept, they worshiped, and they rejoiced. (See Neh. 8:1-12.)

So significant was this rereading of the Law that Israel's faith became known thereafter as "the religion of the Book."

These stories of books lost then found probably have symbolic significance. Dr. Nibley asserts: "The idea of the holy book that is taken away from the earth and restored from time to time, or is handed down secretly from father to son for generations, or hidden up in the earth, preserved by ingenious methods of storage with precious imperishable materials to be brought forth in a later and more righteous generation (e.g., Moses 1:41) is becoming increasingly familiar with the discovery and publication of ever more ancient apocryphal works."[12]

In other words, the lost-then-found status of the Israelites' ancient records is part of a historical pattern and has a close relationship to the righteousness of the generations to which the records are given.

The Completion of the Old Testament Records

Ezra's reading is believed to have been the first time interpreters were needed to turn the writings into the spoken language of the people: the book was written in Hebrew, but after the captivity the people spoke Aramaic. Some also believe it was Ezra who began a collection of official Hebrew scriptures after the Babylonian captivity and during the time of Nehemiah. (Latter-day Saints know there was at least one such collection—the brass plates—which Lehi took with him prior to the captivity.) Evidently Ezra's work was to begin to gather the records of his people. It was an extremely important and demanding task to collect, sort, rewrite, and finally compile many records into one. Because of this work some have called Ezra a second Moses.

The exact procedure by which some of the many Israelite writings became scripture is too uncertain and too complex to cover here, but scholars agree upon three basic steps. The foundation, of course, was the Pentateuch, historically first and always considered the first in importance. Next to be added, and also therefore the next in importance were works by and about the prophets, which included the historical books. Historical books were included as prophecy because they were written by prophets and because the history in them was considered prophetic.

But it would be a great mistake to think it was easy for the works of all the prophets to win a place in the Hebrews' hearts as scriptures. One scholar claims, "At first the validity of the teaching of prophets like Amos, Hosea, Isaiah, Micah, Jeremiah, and Ezekiel was recognized only by the faithful disciples who learned from them and transmitted the traditions of what they had said and done."[13] These writings did not receive wide public acknowledgement until during and after the exile. What caused this change in status? Very simply, these prophets had prophesied of the fall of Jerusalem and of the Babylonian captivity. After the fact, when the people had seen that their words had come to pass, they accepted these men in remorse and repentance as true prophets whose words were worthy to be placed among the sacred scriptures.

An example of the rejection the prophets and their writings experienced before the captivity is seen in the life of Jeremiah. In the year before the coming of Babylon, the Lord commanded Jeremiah to write the prophecies he had been speaking. So Jeremiah dictated to his scribe, Baruch, his witness "against Israel, and against Judah." Because Jeremiah had been forbidden to preach any more at the temple, Baruch took the roll and read it at the temple on a special day when many were assembled. News of the scroll reached King Jehoiakim, who asked for a reading—but not with willing ears. As the words were read, he cut the scroll with a knife and disdainfully cast it into the fire.

Although the king also sought to harm Jeremiah and Baruch, they escaped and were commanded by God to write a second roll containing all the words of the first and more. It is believed that we have obtained our book of Jeremiah from this writing. (See Jer. 36.)

Behind the writings of all the prophets were similar trials, sufferings, and accusations. Most were rejected, mocked, scorned. Some were accused as the "troublers of Israel." Jeremiah was for a time cast into a deep dungeon where he lay in mire and was given only bread to eat. Jewish and Christian traditions hold that Isaiah was encased within a tree trunk and sawn asunder and that the deed was done at the instigation of Manasseh, King of Judah.

Many prophets, such as Ezekiel, who forewarned the people of impending captivity and exile, did not escape that fate themselves but experienced the same sufferings as their people. Yet out of that suffering they prophesied and wrote of the days when God's people would again be released and redeemed.

Just as the prophetic utterances of these prophets were only belatedly recognized, by 200 B.C. the people began to believe that all prophecy had ceased. Consequently, there was little "prophecy" added to the sacred collection. There is now evidence that prophets continued to actively teach; but most of the people, never comprehending their true needs, believed they had all of the scriptures they needed, and rejected the thought of more.

Last to win a place among the sacred collection were the "Writings," works such as Psalms, Proverbs, Job, and Esther. Although accepted into the collection, the "Writings" never equalled the first two sections in importance in the eyes of Jewish leaders. Of this group, only the Psalms were used in worship, although many of the "Writings" came to be traditionally read at various religious festivals.

The order in which the books appear in our present Old Testament is not the order in which they were written, nor the exact order in which they were accepted as canon. The current arrangement follows that of the Septuagint (which will be discussed later), which uses a pattern based on subject matter: Law, History, Poetry, Prophecy. This system is claimed to be educational, since it traces the progress of revelation. First it relates events of the past (Law and History); then the poetic books speak of things pertaining to their own time; finally the books of prophecy, although delivering a contemporary message, are perceived as speaking to the future.

Of course many writings for some reason did not make it at all into the completed canon. We know there were others because the writers of our books refer as resources to the books of Jasher, of Samuel the Seer, of Nathan the prophet, of Jehu, and of the Kings of Israel. The reasons each was excluded are unknown.

Thus, the works and words of Israel's prophets gradually were shaped into a record. But the birth process was scarcely painless. Jeremiah most poignantly recorded the great burden of being mouthpiece for the Lord. "Oh Lord, . . . I am in derision daily, every one mocketh me. For since I spake, I cried out, I cried violence and spoil; because the word of the Lord was made a reproach unto me, and a derision, daily. Then I said, I will not make mention of him, nor speak any more in his name. But his word was in mine heart as a burning fire shut up in my bones, and I was weary with forbearing, and I could not stay." (Jer. 20:7-9.)

CHAPTER TWO

The Word Is Preserved

There were several ways to record and preserve records anciently—none of them easy. The most common was to use papyrus, called by some a creation of genius because of its weightlessness, its strength, its flexibility, its portability, and its storageability. Papyrus was made from pith scraped from the papyrus plant, then wetted and pressed together. Scribes could write on both the front and back. For more space, additional scrolls could be pasted at the bottom, the whole being rolled around rods. One roll still in existence is as long as one hundred and forty-four feet!

Clay tablets were also written upon and then baked in the sun or in kilns. More durable than papyrus, clay tablets are more commonly discovered in ancient ruins.

Records were also made upon writing boards—flat boards of wood or ivory whose center was carved out and replaced with an inlay of wax, which could be written upon. The boards were hinged together to become a folding book. Surely this is the kind of record to which Ezekiel is referring when he speaks of writing upon the two sticks of Judah and Ephraim. (See Ezek. 37:16-17.)

Animal skin (leather) was also used by the Hebrews. In fact, a Jewish tradition indicates that anything as sacred as the Torah had to be written on leather. But for significant religious records metals were also used.

While we can mention all those methods quite easily in passing, we do the ancient scribes injustice if we do not at least acknowledge the great hand labor required to prepare these writing materials before even one letter could ever be set down upon them.

The preservation of records was of great concern to the Hebrews. From the first, scriptures were treated with the utmost care: Moses' writings were preserved in the ark of the covenant. The scriptures record the names of those who were called to be state scribes, for this was considered an office of great importance. Senior scribes were even given their own rooms in the palaces and temples. Ancient writings remained only in the hands of priests and were read only by scribes. Each scroll had to be copied directly from another scroll, and until the destruction of the temple, official copies were taken directly from the master copy in the temple. The official scrolls were the holiest objects in the synagogue and were treated in every way like treasures.

New scribes were carefully instructed about the sacredness of their task: "My son, be careful in thy work, for it is heavenly work, lest thou err in omitting or in adding one jot [the smallest letter in the Hebrew alphabet] and so cause the destruction of the whole world."[1]

To appreciate more fully the sacrifices that have gone into producing our Bible, we must touch upon the difficulties of writing in biblical times. The earliest biblical writers probably lived and worked in tents. The people of the Near East did not have furniture as we know it—they sat cross-legged upon the ground on mats or cushions. This continued into Roman times. From the Egyptians have come representations of how some ancient scribes worked. There is a replica of one scribe seated upon the floor in a traditional cross-legged position, his skirt or kilt drawn out so tightly by his legs that the skirt itself serves as a desk to hold his roll of papyrus and to write upon.[2]

The scribe of the Near East usually worked under intense heat, often sitting for many hours in the same position. The work also required a considerable amount of solitude in order to avoid distractions.

The profession, though, commanded respect. In ancient Egypt the scribe was described as "the taskmaster of everyone." And in encouraging a son to become a good scribe, an Egyptian bureaucrat said, "It is to writings that you must set your mind. . . . I do not see an office to be compared with [that of the scribe]. . . . I shall make you love books more than your mother, and I shall place their excellence before you."[3]

Style and Form

While dealing with the actual techniques of writing, something should be said about its more important counterpart—the art or style of writing used in the Old Testament. For the scriptures are far more than just history: they contain the word of the Lord. As such, they deserve to be put into the most beautiful setting possible; and, for the most part, they were. Although each writer spoke out of his own time and culture and in spite of his own weaknesses, each spoke with a flair. Their record is not merely prose, but rhythmic prose, and often even poetry. In fact, several of the prophetic books are in part or almost wholly poetic, though we may not recognize this at first, for Hebrew poetry differs from English poetry. Hebrew poetry, rather than using a repetition of sounds for effectiveness, achieves its impact through rhythmic repetition and balance of ideas, either similar or contrasting.

The effect of the style used by the prophets is to carry truth to the ear in a more powerful, more pleasing, more memorable way. Calling the Old Testament style exquisite in beauty, one writer said that the Hebrew prophets were all "touched by the magic of poetic genius, with an unmatched gift for language and imagery."[4] Imagine, to be prophet and poet both!

But surely poetic form did not come readily. We can only imagine the many additional hours, the greater patience and exertion required to work and rework the scriptures until the form was rhythmic and the imagery and language poetic.

But we are the blessed recipients of the results. Genesis is declared a great work of genius and "one of the noblest literary

and religious monuments ever produced by the hand of man."[5]
Of Isaiah's writings it is said that "Beauty and strength are
characteristic of his entire book. He is a perfect artist in words,"
and that "Every word from him stirs and strikes its mark."[6]
Of the Psalms it is said they reflect "the soul experiences of the
whole race of mankind."[7] Of Job, that its writer possessed a
"penetrating, rich, daring, and creative mind."[8]

The Hebrew writers were indeed literary artists of great
stature, so great in fact that modern scholars are still discovering
the strengths of their work. The incredible art form of chiasmus
in which ideas are intricately reversed as if a mirror were held
up to them is a fairly recent discovery. An extremely complex
and unified structure, layer upon layer, in the writings of Isaiah
has recently been shown by Avraham Gileadi.[9]

The Hebrew writers also used skillful plays on words, by
which words took on double meanings, and their prophecies
were also skillfully arranged to carry double meanings. They
often spoke of a current or near-future event, blending into it
prophecies of a parallel far-future event.[10]

One writer says that the Hebrews "possessed a concrete
directness of thought, a clarity of vision, an instinct for synthe-
sis, and an appreciation of reality, which made them ideal expo-
nents of truth for simple people. And they had a great and
stately music in their soul."[11]

But the most incredible quality about the Hebrew scriptures
is that it is a history saturated with similitudes—or enacted,
living types of Christ, the ultimate Suffering Servant. That is
to say, some of the Hebrew authors not only *wrote about*, but
also *portrayed through their lives* future prophecies.

Abraham was asked to offer a son as sacrifice; Moses struggled through a wilderness as savior to a rebellious and spiritually
blind people. Job was a righteous man persecuted and accused
by his friends as a sinner. Jeremiah's friends and family also
opposed him, and he was "doomed to preach an unwelcome
message, while the false prophets persuaded the people that
he was unpatriotic, uninspired, and pessimistic."[12] And his
descent into a pit and mire and his reascension paralleled
Christ's death and resurrection. Hosea also is described as "little
less than a martyr, prefiguring Christ."[13]

Only when we realize that the prophets' greatest contribution to the word of God was the lives they led can we fully grasp just how much they really gave for the sake of truth.

The Challenges of Translation

Once the scriptures were written, there developed a continual challenge of keeping them accessible to the people whose language sometimes changed. Aramaic is generally thought to have been the general tongue of the Hebrews after their Babylonian captivity. Since it was also the language used in trade and diplomatic relations over a wide area, it became entrenched as the everyday speech of the inhabitants of Judah. Therefore, from the fourth century B.C., the Hebrew scriptures were an enigma for most Jews unless translated for them. Yet at that point, according to Jewish tradition, written translations were forbidden, as if the language and the concepts were inseparable. Oral translations were permitted, but only by official synagogue translators. Even then, the translation had to be done verse by verse in the Torah and at least after every third verse in the "Prophets."[14]

The oral translations, or Targums, were more than just translations. They were often used for interpretation and explanation. The religious leaders found these methods useful in overcoming what they felt were misunderstood passages. An example used by one scholar of explanatory translation is that given for Exodus 24:10, which states, "And they saw the God of Israel." In Aramaic it was interpreted, "And they saw the glory of the God of Israel."[15] It is particularly interesting that the passages indicating an anthropomorphic (physical) God were the ones most often explained away. Not surprisingly then, when One arrived a few centuries later claiming to be the Son of God, his claim was met with hostility: the rejection of a God with a material body had begun long before.

Eventually, *written* Targums were also allowed, but the translations had to be written between the lines of the Hebrew on the scrolls. Translation into Aramaic became quite extensive: remnants of Targums of almost all the books of the Old Testament have been discovered.

But there was a need for other translations as well. With

the conquest of Palestine by Alexander the Great in 333 B.C., the Jews were again dispersed, this time to Egypt. Once again, many who adapted themselves to living in other lands never returned. Now there were two major centers of the Diaspora (scattering): Babylon and Alexandria. Alexander's conquests had spread the use of Greek throughout a very wide area, and Greek became the language used in commercial and literary enterprises. Most Jews living in lands other than Judah became Greek-speaking.

And so around 250 B.C. a translation was made of the Hebrew scriptures into Greek, but not initially for the Jews. According to Josephus this translation occurred under the reign of King Ptolemy of Egypt and because his library keeper desired to accumulate all the books of the civilized world, including the writings of the Jews. A letter was written to the Jewish high priest requesting the records and translators. Jewish slaves were released and gifts sent as inducement.

In response, six elders out of every tribe (or seventy-two) went to Egypt to translate. Of particular interest in Josephus's story is the admiration the Egyptian king showed when he saw the fine Jewish records, written in gold letters upon "membranes" (interpreted "parchments"): "So the king stood admiring the thinness of those membranes, and the exactness of the junctures, which could not be perceived, (so exactly were they connected one with another;) and this he did for considerable time."[16]

Josephus summarizes the work of translating simply: "They made an accurate interpretation, with great zeal and great pains; and this they continued to do till the ninth hour of the day."[17] Though it is surprising, more than one source attributes the completion time of the work to seventy-two days. Because of the elements of seventy—seventy-two scholars and seventy-two days—the work came to be known as the Septuagint, which means Seventy, or Version of the Seventy.

The Septuagint was well accepted by the Jews of Alexandria and later became a powerful influence in the world.

We can see then that the Hebrews have given much in the way of writing, copying, and translating these sacred records known as the Old Testament. But there was also a great cost in

THE WORD IS PRESERVED

preservation. Around 175 B.C., when the Greek ruler Antiochus came into power, he turned upon the Judeans in a fury. He sacked Jerusalem, pulling down a portion of the walls. He altogether forbid the practice of Judaism, demanding the cessation of sacrifice and circumcision and ordered that their "Law" be burned.

In general, the Jews determinedly resisted. They continued their sacred worship, submitting to slaughter by the sword rather than forsaking it. Above all, they refused to relinquish their holy writings. "Men clung to their Torahs as to life itself, and ended by surrendering both."[18]

The Old Testament during the Time of Christ

The record of the Jews, though sparse in parts, had been built step by step from the time of Adam. It had grown to a collection of many sacred writings and had been translated into the changing common languages of the people. But now its very Author, the One from whom it had all originally sprung, appeared upon the scene. The scriptures themselves relate this wondrous happening: "In the beginning was the Word, . . . and the Word was God. . . . And the Word was made flesh, and dwelt among us." (John 1:1, 14.)

He who from the beginning had uttered the words that prophets had written and man had studied and vocalized and repeated—he of whom all the scriptures had borne witness— came among his people. Sitting in the seats of power and influence at that time were men who had obtained their positions through bribery and political appointment. To these rulers who possessed his words but understood them not he said, "Ye do err, not knowing the scriptures." (Matt. 22:29.) Of these rulers who possessed his words but did them not, he said, "The scribes and the Pharisees sit in Moses' seat: all therefore whatsoever they bid you observe, that observe and do; but do not ye after their works: for they say, and do not." (Matt 23:2-3.) And finally, through the hands of these same rulers, his word was accomplished: his atonement, crucifixion, and resurrection were the fulfillment of all that the writings had taught.

After his resurrection, he showed his disciples how the Old Testament had borne witness of all the events that had just come to pass. On the road to Emmaus those who walked with him exclaimed, "Did not our heart burn within us, . . . while he opened to us the scriptures?" (Luke 24:32.) Then he departed, and his disciples were left to take the joyful news that the old word—the laws, prophecies, and covenants—had been fulfilled through Christ's life, death, and resurrection.

The basic scripture of the earliest Christians was the Septuagint, the Hebrew record translated into Greek. But the record was used in a new way—as a witness to Christ. It was in this role that the Septuagint began to play a vital part. When the Christian message began to spread outside the borders of Palestine, the Septuagint became the main instrument of teaching and conversion. Already in the international tongue of Greek, it allowed a rapid spreading of the gospel to many nations. (And interestingly, its name, *Septuagint*, takes on new meaning: it became a missionary—a seventy—to all the nations.)

Several incidents in the New Testament detail conversions occurring through the use of the Old Testament. One missionary, Apollos, "mightily convinced the Jews, and that publickly, shewing by the scriptures [the Old Testament] that Jesus was Christ." (Acts 18:28.)

The Hebrew records, then, were not abandoned by the first Christians. Rather, they were studied even more diligently, but with new eyes. Unlike the unconverted Jews, who believed their records contained all, Christians (both Jewish and gentile) were taught that they contained but the first step—testaments that would lead to new life through the Savior.

Just as there emerged vast differences in the way Jew and Christian interpreted the ancient writings, so there were some differences in the actual manuscripts they used. There are differences in the wording found in Greek and Hebrew scrolls. The Septuagint's "a virgin shall conceive" was "a young woman" in the later Masoretic version. Exactly how and at what point differences emerged is not firmly established.[19]

In addition, early Christian apostles made references to teachings found in writings attributed to Moses and Enoch but which are not found in scriptures possessed by traditional Judaism. Various manuscripts discovered in modern times claim that after his resurrection Christ himself gave his Apostles certain ancient writings the Jews didn't possess.[20]

After the Time of Christ

The fact that Christ's followers utilized the Septuagint so extensively was greatly disturbing to rabbinic Jews. Disavowing the Septuagint, these Jews prepared translations of the Greek that were more acceptable to them, making references to a material God less obvious.[21] And they interpreted some messianic prophecies far differently from those in the Septuagint.[22]

Many events at this time had devastating impact upon the Jews: the rise of Christianity, which, to them, was a major apostasy; Christianity's misappropriation of their scriptures; the fall of Jerusalem; and the second destruction of the temple. These events caused them to reexamine the status of their records. Since the temple, their central place of worship, had again been destroyed, they became even more "the religion of the book," for the book was the only religious thing of a physical nature left to them.[23]

Sometime during the first century the Jews made a final determination of what constituted authoritative Jewish scriptures. There is evidence that the Council of Jamnia in A.D. 90 may have been the culmination of this effort, for the council debated the authority of certain books and established a fixed canon of Judaic writings.[24] Among books not included were some accepted by Christians. Apocalyptic writings, in particular, were the ones most consistently discriminated against and have survived (except for Daniel and parts of Ezekiel, Isaiah, and Zechariah) only in noncanonical works.[25]

To ensure thereafter that the canon would be preserved uniformly, all future Hebrew manuscripts were made to conform to a certain pattern, and variant texts were destroyed or suppressed.[26]

Much of the work of preserving the Hebrew scriptures through the centuries after Christ was accomplished by the Masoretes, traditional Jewish scholars who worked in Palestine and Babylon between the sixth and tenth centuries A.D. The Hebrew manuscript with which they dealt was a *solid mass of consonants:* there were no written vowels, no word separations, no punctuation. The tedious work of transcribing and the lack of space had led Hebrew scribes to utilize this shorthand system. Regarding the text as sacred, the Masoretes were reluctant to insert vowels, but they developed a system of using dots and dashes which *stood* for certain vowels. In essence, they were filling out the words without changing the consonantal text.[27]

The copying methods of the Masoretes were strictly prescribed by Talmudic law. Among the rules were the following: (1) A synagogue roll had to be written on skins of clean animals prepared specifically by a synagogue Jew. (2) Only authentic copies were to be recopied, and scribes were not to deviate in the least. (3) Nothing must be written from memory.[28]

For years, scholars searching for original copies of our scriptures were unable to find any Old Testament copies in Hebrew older than the ninth century A.D. Part of the reason for this is that as new copies were made, the old were burned or buried.[29] Though parts of some manuscripts eventually turned up, the real breakthrough came in the 1940s when the Dead Sea Scrolls were discovered. Among the scrolls were one of Isaiah and portions of all other Old Testament books excluding Esther. Although they agree generally with later copies, there are also important points of divergence, enough to arouse some belief that they were taken from different original texts.[30] So while our Old Testament has been canonized and theoretically completed, scholars perpetually seek for its sources and for its original texts hoping to reconcile all differences.

Regardless of its failings, the Old Testament as preserved by the Jews deserves high tribute. It is praised by scholars of many faiths. Some point out that unlike the tales of other Near Eastern cultures, archaeological evidence shows that Israel's story is true history and deserves praise for its respect for fact— particularly since respect for fact did not generally prevail during the time of its writing. Others point out that while neighboring cultures had records of beliefs and ways of life, these beliefs died and are known now only because of excavations centuries later.

But the Jewish history and record of beliefs, far from dying and being buried, "has provided a continuing tradition and a source of constant study; people have read it, re-examined it and lived by it."[31]

One writer, in describing the effect the writings of the book have had upon the Jewish people through the centuries has said:

> "Not always, indeed not often, were [the prophets] successful in their immediate purpose. But . . . [through all,] the people were still receptive to an appeal to the spirit and uncommonly endowed with a reverence for the word . . . Even when they failed at the time to heed what they heard, they at least delighted in the exhortation of their poet-prophets. They savoured them, relished them and repeated them, and — usually when catastrophe followed non-compliance — remembered them, and handed them on from generation to generation. . . . Venerated, read and studied by every successive Jewish generation, [the books] contained the supreme code of Jewish life, gave the Jews their specific religion and identity, and preserved them as a people, nourishing their hopes at all times, sobering them in their triumphs, encouraging them in their trials, guiding and sustaining them throughout all the centuries of their vicissitudes."[32]

Thus, from the beginning, the word went forth from God. Men received it and sought to hold on to it. Though some was lost, much was saved. Our eighth article of faith recognizes this fact, and yet it also affirms the record's divine origin, counseling that it be read with an ear tuned to the voice of the Spirit. Although we look forward to the time when the records will be whole, what we now have is reverenced and appreciated.

It is a good foundation upon which many things have been and will yet be built.

CHAPTER THREE

A New Word Is Added to the Old

Because of the Jews, the Christians from the beginning possessed a body of scriptures as a unique heritage. But unlike orthodox Jews, who believed the collection to be *completed* scripture, Christ's disciples knew there was now a richer portion. They didn't abandon the Old Word, for new understanding had made it more precious than ever. But they now had a New Word as well—Christ's teachings and the powerful example and acts of his life.

The testimonies that have come to us of this New Word are those of apostles or of disciples closely associated with apostles: Matthew, Mark, Luke, and John. Several ancient sources confirm that the gospel bearing the name of Matthew was written by the apostle Matthew, otherwise called Levi, the tax collector, who is said to have been run through with a spear as a consequence of his written and oral testimony.

Matthew spoke powerfully to his own people, longing for their eyes to be opened so they could see that the man Jesus fulfilled the Old Testament prophecies and was their long-expected Messiah. His testimony is sweetened by many direct quotations of the Savior's own words. It is Matthew to whom we are indebted for a detailed recounting of Christ's Sermon on the Mount. In fact, there is a recorded statement by a bishop named Papias in the first half of the second century that Matthew was the one who compiled a record of Christ's sayings in Hebrew, and that others used his record as a source for their own testimonies of Christ's life and teachings.[1]

The testimony of Mark may be in a sense the testimony of Peter, for Mark was Peter's interpreter, and the relationship was so close Peter referred to him as "son." There is some evidence that Mark made his record under Peter's guidance and authority. The same bishop Papias wrote that Mark traveled with Peter and recorded the things Peter taught about Christ's life and teachings.[2]

Mark, then, strongly reflecting Peter's testimony, portrayed Christ mostly in his mission as Redeemer, the *acts* of Christ's life being his major focus. It is generally agreed his testimony was to the gentiles. His message was that Christ could heal the deaf, the blind, the lame and could redeem those bound in sin, that he had been resurrected and thereby had overcome death for all. A spiritually hungry gentile world needed such knowledge and hope.

The Gospel of Luke and the Acts of the Apostles were both written by Luke, a close companion of Paul (Acts 16:10, 20:6; 2 Tim. 4:11), and therefore bear Paul's influence. But the authority behind Luke's account is also derived from Luke's claim to be a messenger of the Savior and to have sought original sources, the witnesses of the original apostles themselves and other eyewitnesses. (See JST Luke 1:1-4.)

Many see Luke's testimony as emphasizing the universality of Christ's mission. He traces Christ's lineage clear back to Adam, perhaps as witness that Christ has relationship to all mankind. Since Luke's testimony includes both his gospel and the book of Acts, his account is more complete, disclosing Christianity's history from its humble birth in Bethlehem to its struggles to survive in Rome. Since Luke traveled extensively with Paul, he was able to recount not only Christ's life but the birth pangs of the church itself as it began to spread into the world.

John's gospel stands alone, the tenor of its content unique. According to the Book of Mormon, John was given a special calling pertaining to the Book of the Lamb of God. Nephi writes:

"And I looked and beheld a man, and he was dressed in a white robe. And the angel said unto me: Behold one of the twelve apostles of the Lamb. Behold, he shall see and write the remainder of these things [Nephi had been shown highlights of Christ's life]; yea, and also many things which have been. And he shall also write concerning the end of the world. . . . But the things which thou shalt see hereafter thou shalt not write; for the Lord God hath ordained the apostle of the Lamb of God that he should write them.

"And I, Nephi, heard and bear record, that the name of the apostle of the Lamb was John, according to the word of the angel." (1 Ne. 14:19-22, 25, 27.)

It is interesting that for a time the gospel of John was a work whose authenticity was attacked most strongly by scholars of the higher criticism. Yet in modern times more fragments of John in ancient form have been found than any of the synoptic gospels, and its great worth is becoming more widely recognized.

Part of the difference in John's gospel is that he wrote it to members of the church. Therefore, he spoke on a higher plane, giving deeper understanding to things already known. He reaffirmed above all else that Christ was indeed God who had taken upon himself flesh, saying, "These are written, that ye might believe that Jesus is the Christ, the son of God; and that believing ye might have life through his name." (John 20:31.)

It was John who, listening to the Savior's teachings, was more sensitive to their symbolic meanings. It was he who recorded for us that Jesus Christ was the lamb who would be slain for us, the bread from heaven who would nourish us, the light that would enlighten us, the vine from which we could draw strength and through which we might bear fruit. And finally, it was John generally who revealed some of the most intimate of Christ's teachings, those given just to his apostles, as at the last supper and after his resurrection.

The first and the best texts of the New Testament, then, like those of the Old, came from the prophets, either by their own hands or by the hands of very close assistants, somewhat like apostolic scribes.

We see too, because Christ is viewed from many different angles or perspectives, that each writer of a gospel distinctly adds to the overall picture. Indeed, there are some special values in having four different accounts of Christ's life. While there are some dissimilarities and numerous theories as to why they exist, we must remember there is much more unity than disunity. As A. R. Fausset points out in a Reader's Bible Aid, "Reconcilable diversity is a confirmation of truth, because it disproves collusion, and shews the witnesses to be independent. Sameness in all four gospels would make all but the first mere copies."[3]

Of course for some time a number of scholars have not accepted the gospels as having come from the apostles or from the apostolic period, believing they were written quite some time after the actual events. However, discovery of the Dead Sea Scrolls shows that extensive literary activity was a part of that period and most likely was a part of the new Christian movement as well. For Latter-day Saints, who have been taught that the Lord with care provided from the beginning for a record of his work among men, and who know that he carefully instructed his Nephite followers during his visit to them to make records of his sayings, it would be very difficult to believe that he did not make provisions for the recording of his Palestine teachings and for his acts of atonement, crucifixion, and resurrection, particularly since he intended the gospel to go to all the world for succeeding generations. The only way that could be accomplished efficiently would be through written records.

While we must offer high praise to the writers of the four gospels, who labored greatly in a period of severe persecution to preserve for us these precious accounts, we must also recognize the greater gift behind them—from the Savior himself. His gift of his incredible life was the "raw material" to which the gospel writers gave written shape. *He was the Word!* He was the Old Word being fulfilled, and he was the New Word being lived. This "greatest story ever told" did not spring from someone's imagination; rather, its impact and power are inescapably bound to its reality—and more so because it was *deliberately lived,* even to its utmost bitterness:

"After this, Jesus knowing that all things were now accomplished, that the scripture might be fulfilled, saith, I thirst.

Now there was set a vessel full of vinegar: and they filled a spunge with vinegar, and put it upon hyssop, and put it to his mouth. When Jesus therefore had received the vinegar, he said, It is finished: and he bowed his head, and gave up the ghost. . . .

"But when [the soldiers] came to Jesus, . . . one of the soldiers with a spear pierced his side, and forthwith came there out blood and water. . . . For these things were done, that the scripture should be fulfilled, A bone of him shall not be broken. And again another scripture saith, They shall look on him whom they pierced." (John 19:28-30, 33-34, 36-37.)

Christ's contributions to the strength of the New Testament can also be seen in his spoken word. One writer says, "When speaking to a group and with prophetic fervor [Christ's] discourse would be marked with intensity and rhythm not dissimilar to poetical passages in the Old Testament prophets."[4]

As the Old Testament had been established step by step, so the New Testament had begun to grow. The book *The Bible through the Ages* claims that apparently the four gospels were united in time into a four-gospel scroll manuscript. Some believe that because Matthew was the most popular, it was placed first. We know more certainly that by A.D. 170 there were codices (or books) available containing the gospels, Acts, and Paul's letters.[5] It appears however that other gospels were written by other apostles. Manuscripts of writings claiming to be such have become more widely known and available in recent years. There undoubtedly were such gospels. The problems are finding them in pure form and ascertaining true authorship. The whole problem of materials corrupted or lost altogether from the record was prophesied in the Book of Mormon, as was the eventual influence of this growing body of writings.

> The angel said unto me [Nephi]: Knowest thou the meaning of the book?
> And I said unto him: I know not.
> And he said: Behold it proceedeth out of the mouth of a Jew. And I, Nephi, beheld it; and he said unto me: The book that thou beholdest is a record of the Jews, which contains the covenants of the Lord, which he hath made unto the house of Israel; and it also containeth many of the prophecies of the holy prophets; and it is a record like unto the engravings

which are upon the plates of brass, save there are not so many; nevertheless, they contain the covenants of the Lord, which he hath made unto the house of Israel; wherefore, they are of great worth unto the Gentiles.

And the angel of the Lord said unto me: Thou hast beheld that the book proceeded forth from the mouth of a Jew; and when it proceeded forth from the mouth of a Jew it contained the fulness of the gospel of the Lord, of whom the twelve apostles bear record; and they bear record according to the truth which is in the Lamb of God. Wherefore, these things go forth from the Jews in purity unto the Gentiles, according to the truth which is in God.

And after they go forth by the hand of the twelve apostles of the Lamb, from the Jews unto the Gentiles, thou seest the formation of that great and abominable church . . . ; for behold, they [the Gentiles] have taken away from the gospel of the Lamb many parts which are plain and most precious. (1 Ne. 13:20-26.)

There are indeed many witnesses that a far larger body of literature from the early Christian period existed than we now have in our possession. In fact, it is amazing just how sparse our record really is. While the four testimonies that bear witness of Christ's life do so with much power, they do not cover the greater part of his life. In Mark's story, for example, only thirty-one days are accounted for. Furthermore, in the New Testament the total sayings attributed to Christ can be read in one hour. When one considers the numerous occasions that he taught, and the times his sermons extended well into the day or the evening, we realize that only a very small portion of his teachings has survived.

But the real gap in the New Testament accounts is the period after the resurrection. We know that at that time Christ spent forty days with his apostles—forty days in which he expanded upon his word. How vital those teachings and instructions must have been! Yet they are almost totally missing from our current New Testament.

Also, as we know, after the Gospels and the Acts of the Apostles, much of the New Testament consists of a collection of letters. Having so much of the New Testament in letter form has proved both a strength and a problem for Christianity. The strengths are pointed out by Richard L. Anderson, who shows that beyond their value for spiritual upliftment, the letters help verify the accuracy of the history and the doctrine expressed in the Gospels.[6]

On the other hand, because of the loss of precious knowledge from the New Testament texts, the letters have had to assume a role for which they were never intended. The Gospels as we have them focus primarily on the life of Christ, on those teachings that bear witness that he is the Christ, and on his teachings about how man ought to live. They do not contain a complete presentation of the full range of gospel doctrines and principles. Generally, therefore, Christian sects have obtained many of their doctrines from the epistles. But the epistles themselves, though they contain doctrine, do so in patches and pieces. Most of them were written in response to specific needs and questions arising in specific geographical areas of the early Church.

Furthermore, some were quite informal or personal, and though sometimes their authors requested that they be read in church, for the most part the authors probably did not intend for their letters to be bound as scriptures. In addition, the letters often contained many items of unequal weight and importance. Basic knowledge of the gospel was presumed to exist among the early Church congregations, so details of many gospel principles were left out of the epistles. Thus, many things were only alluded to, such as baptism for the dead and the roles of the various priesthood leaders. It is this partial explanation that has caused confusion for later readers. In fact, it could be argued that this unfortunate lack of clarity of doctrine is largely responsible for many of the later divisions of belief among Christian sects.

But though we grieve for what was lost, we can still rejoice in what we have in the New Testament record. In spite of its imperfections, this record alone, as the "Book of the Lamb of God," has the honor of detailing the sacrifices and sufferings of Jesus the Christ. It alone contains the power of Christ's mortal living example and the majority of Christ's earthly teachings. Even fragments of the gospels are precious for what they contain—and for how we received them. Almost always, behind every worthy piece of literature there is a fascinating story. And with the knowledge that revelation never comes easily, the stories behind the formation of *scripture* surely would prove to be the most fascinating of all.

Unfortunately, in most cases we know little of the specifics of those forces that pressed upon each New Testament writer and brought from his pen God's word. But we know that the things Christ prophesied to them would come to their minds later. We know on the eve of his death he warned that they would be hated, they would be persecuted, they would be cast out of their own synagogues, and they would be slain. Early Christian writings and tradition affirm that these warnings were realized. Clement of Rome wrote that before their deaths the apostles suffered much. "By reason of rivalry and envy the greatest and most righteous pillars [of the Church] were persecuted, and battered to the death. . . . Peter, who by reason of wicked jealousy, not only once or twice but frequently endured suffering and thus, bearing his witness, went to the glorious place which he merited. By reason of rivalry and contention Paul showed how to win the prize for patient endurance."[7]

Because we possess a more prolific and personal set of writings from Paul, we can learn through his experiences a little of what all must have endured. Paul's insights and writings were spawned by experience. He could write, then, of the miracle of Christ's grace because he had personally experienced it. He had set himself upon a course of crushing the seeds of Christianity, only to be turned from pursuit of that disastrous course by the direct intervention of the Lord. The weight of that indebtedness was one reason he accepted so readily his appointed missions to unknown lands and people, everywhere preaching and writing of the salvation that comes through Christ.

But the strengths of Paul's writings came from other influences as well. In his labors he experienced stonings, scourgings, mockings, illness, and accusations. He faced death many times, and his escapes were narrow. His traveling for the word was constant. He was shipwrecked. He knew loneliness. Like Christ, he was deserted by friends. He was accused, chained, imprisoned—with imprisonments as long as two years. He was tried again and again, finally condemned, and at last martyred.

Out of all these experiences came his letters. He wrote when he suffered "trouble, as an evil doer, even unto bonds" (2 Tim. 2:9); nevertheless he could rise up and say, "But I determined this with myself, that I would not come again to you in heaviness" (2 Cor. 2:1). And he wrote, "We were pressed out of measure, above strength, insomuch that we despaired even of life." (2 Cor. 1:8.) And finally he submissively wrote, "For I am now ready to be offered, and the time of my departure is at hand." (2 Tim. 4:6.)

While in prison, he pleaded for his scriptures: "The cloke that I left . . . , when thou comest, bring with thee, and the books, but especially the parchments." (2 Tim. 4:13.) He loved the scriptures, and in his loving, wrote scripture: "From a child thou hast known the holy scriptures, which are able to make thee wise unto salvation through faith which is in Christ Jesus. All scripture is given by inspiration of God, and is profitable for doctrine, for reproof, for correction, for instruction in righteousness: that the man of God may be perfect." (2 Tim. 3:15-17.)

As Paul spoke of the writings he so greatly loved, so in time his writings have come to be greatly loved, as are the writings of all his companions who bore witness through pen of their faith in Jesus Christ. Though we know more of Paul's trials, he surely spoke for all who used the pen to spread the gospel when he said, "For out of much affliction and anguish of heart I wrote unto you with many tears." (2 Cor. 2:4.)

The Book of Revelation, written by John, began also in a period and place of sorrow—from a lonely exile on a barren rock: "I John, who also am your brother, and companion in tribulation, . . . was in the isle that is called Patmos, for the word of God, and for the testimony of Jesus Christ." (Rev. 1:9.) Undoubtedly more powerful even than the physical isolation and loneliness that surrounded John was the spiritual isolation he suffered. We can sense it as we read his words. For John did not write in a time of success, but of gloom. He was probably the sole remaining apostle in the Old World, and he deeply grieved over the terrible deaths of so many he cherished. The young struggling kingdom was beset upon from all sides. The saints were hunted, persecuted, and slain. But more distressingly, the Church was being ravished from within by false teachings. Undoubtedly the loneliness and sorrow that burdened John contributed strongly to the passion in his words over the joy of light and hope that flooded him as he saw the revealed, living Christ: "I am he that liveth, and was dead; and, behold, I am alive for evermore, Amen; and have the keys of hell and of death. Write the things which thou hast seen, and the things which are, and the things which shall be hereafter." (Rev. 1:18-19.)

John wrote, as he was commanded and as he was shown, the trials and sufferings and judgments contained in the history of the earth and how all things were inevitably progressing to a glorified kingdom in a glorified world. The contrast of the darkness that he had experienced with the light that he was now experiencing helped turn his record of that vision into powerful, striking literature.

John also saw and revealed his own personal lot of bitterness, which would come to him for the sake of God's word, though it would also be sweet—both initially and ultimately: "I went unto the angel, and said unto him, Give me the little book. And he said unto me, Take it, and eat it up; and it shall make thy belly bitter, but it shall be in thy mouth sweet as honey. And I took the little book out of the angel's hand, and ate it up; and it was in my mouth sweet as honey: and as soon as I had eaten it, my belly was bitter. And he said unto me, Thou must prophesy again before many peoples, and nations, and tongues, and kings." (Rev. 10:9-11.)

Although Revelation is placed at the end of our collection of New Testament scriptures, it is not the last book written. The last written *was* by John, but the distinction of finality for the books of the New Testament goes to his epistles.[8]

One authority comments on this cessation of the writings: "As far as the Biblical Dispensation is concerned, [John I] is probably the last recorded inspired writing of which we have record. After it was penned, the long night of apostate darkness descended upon the earth; the heavens were sealed and God no longer communed with men in open vision and by angelic ministration."[9]

As the testaments of those prophets who bore witness of Christ's coming ceased, so the witnesses of those knowing Christ in the flesh also ceased. Another dispensation had ended. For a time the heavens were shut up and must await another day for the love of God for his needy children to again fling them open.

The Book of the Lamb of God had been written, eventually to be united as an Old Testament and a New Testament. While many cultures have developed and passed on to later generations choice riches, the choicest of all came from the Hebrews.

"[The Hebrews] accomplished little of note in the political or military spheres; their later history was a bitter and unsuccessful struggle for freedom against a series of foreign masters. . . . They left no painting or sculpture behind them, no drama, no epic poetry. What they did leave is a religious literature. . . . [They had] an attitude different from that of all the peoples surrounding them, a conception of divine power and of the government of the universe so simple that to us, who have inherited it from them, it seems obvious, yet in its time so revolutionary that it made them a nation apart, sometimes laughed at, sometimes feared, but always alien."[10]

As Nephi asked, "Have ye obtained a Bible save it were by the Jews?" (2 Ne. 29:6), it would be wise if we all perceived and remembered more poignantly the greatness of this gift of heritage, and the accompanying travails, labors, pains, and diligence of those who recorded their powerful testimonies and therefore helped bring salvation to a dark and dying world.

CHAPTER FOUR

Early Christian Usage of the Scriptures

It should be obvious that all the writings that now make up the New Testament did not jump from men's pens into leather-bound books. As with the Old Testament, the process was slow and piecemeal. Each part was written separately, and those who were fortunate enough to privately possess any scriptures probably, like Paul, would have had separate parchments or scrolls.

Precisely what was accepted as authoritative scriptures by the early Christians is uncertain. Just as the early Christians accepted as authoritative far more Hebrew records than appear in our current Old Testament, so these church members drew upon a body of Christian literature far more extensive than that contained in our current New Testament.[1] The processes by which these manuscripts were sifted, with only some receiving recognition as "canon," occurred at a much later date.[2]

Furthermore, the scriptures they did have were well utilized. Just as the Christians inherited their scriptures from the Jews, so also did they inherit their methods of study and learning from the Jews. As in the synagogue, so in the early Christian meetings was the reading of scriptures a primary part of learning and of worship. In both places, the scriptures held a chief place of honor. To hear them read was a major purpose for attending services.[3] The fact that many members were not literate and could not read them for themselves, and the fact that copies of the scriptures were not readily available to all the members, contributed to this need for central reading.[4]

By the end of the second century A.D., most Christians accepted a list of certain books as authoritative, called them the New Testament, and read them in services along with the Septuagint. Furthermore, they began to appear in codex form (book-like collections of manuscript sheets) rather than on papyrus rolls.[5]

But study and reading also went on in private, where possible. In fact, scripture reading was a central part of a devoted Christian's life. The literate read to the illiterate in the privacy of their homes. Sometimes slaves read to illiterate masters. And some members attributed their conversions to the gospel to such scripture readings.[6]

There is also little doubt that as time passed, the scriptures themselves produced incentive for illiterate Christians to become literate. Indeed, as in Jewish families, scripture study was the basis of a family's education, with study begun when children were yet small. From the earliest time, scripture study had been encouraged by church leaders. Irenaeus (ca. A.D. 120 to 220) wrote, "Let a man take refuge in the Church. Let him be educated in her bosom and be nourished from the Holy Scriptures. . . . Eat ye from every Scripture of the Lord."[7]

The scriptures were memorized as well. Eusebius spoke of a blind man who "possessed whole books of the Holy Scriptures not on tables of stone, . . . nor on skins of beasts or on papyrus . . . but . . . in his heart, so that, as from a rich literary treasure, he could, ever as he wished, repeat now passages from the Law and the Prophets, now from the historical books, now from the Gospels and the Apostolic epistles."[8]

Just as Christians from the outset had recognized that the scriptures were germane to the spiritual well-being of the Church, so also did their enemies. As opponents saw the rapid-fire spread of this new religion, they realized that its books were a key to its destruction. Therefore, as they persecuted and slew the leaders, they also sought to destroy their scriptures.[9] This

persecution, with its accompanying destruction of books, continued through the third century after Christ.[10]

During this time, many scriptures were sought out for destruction, particularly the community caches in the churches.
For protection, the churches appointed certain individuals as
custodians of their scriptural treasures. Betrayal of this responsibility was regarded as a serious transgression, with excommunication its result. While some were unfaithful to their charge
and under pressure betrayed their trust, many more were faithful. Some caches of the scriptures were even buried during
periods of danger, so that they might be preserved.[11]

Another danger, even more insidious, also threatened the
scriptures. While at least some of the scriptures survived the
onslaughts of persecution and burning, holy writ suffered even
further from a change in interpretation.

It is generally conceded that Christ, his apostles, and the
earliest Christian fathers interpreted the Old Testament as continual prophecy of the coming and mission of the Messiah.[12]
One scholar admits, begrudgingly, that "the writings of early
church fathers . . . differ little from that of New Testament authors, in that the Old Testament was regarded as a prediction
of the New Testament and Christ as the fulfillment of Old Testament prophecy."[13] This writer goes on to explain that the
early church fathers saw the Old Testament as "Christian literature," as "parabolic throughout," truly understood only by
Christians because "everything in the Old Testament was a pro-
totype of Christ."[14] Among the writers who used this method
of interpretation were Clement of Rome (A.D. 100), Justin Martyr
(ca. A.D. 155), and Irenaeus (ca. A.D. 200).[15]

Nevertheless, as time passed there were changes in the
methods of interpretation. One individual who exerted a great
influence in changing the interpretation of scripture was the
Christian scholar Origen (A.D. 185-254). While Christ and his
apostles had opened the eyes of the Christians to the concept
that Old Testament events were "types" or foreshadowings of
Him, they never placed in question the basic realities of these
events. But Origen, heavily influenced by Greek thought, came
to feel that many Old Testament events were totally figurative,

that there was no reality behind them. Moreover, he vastly broadened the scope of symbolic interpretation. Rather than seeing Old Testament events as types that taught specifically of Christ, he saw them as more generalized "allegories" with a wide-ranging potential for interpretation. Tragically, this made it easy to read almost anything one wished into the scriptures.[16]

Furthermore, he, like many during his time, rejected the anthropomorphisms in the Bible, asserting that any belief that Moses really saw God must "fall into the absurdity of asserting that God is corporeal."[17] He interpreted scriptural references to immortality as meaning a "spiritual continuity" rather than a "resurrection of the physical body."[18]

However, in addition to these strong and misdirected changes in methods of interpretation, Origen exerted some sound influences upon scriptural studies. He saw a necessity to seek for truly accurate original texts. Beginning a work that took him more than twenty years, called the Hexapla because of its six parts, he made comparisons of the Hebrew, Septuagint, and other Old Testament translations. However, after his death, careless scribes did not include many symbols that kept his procedure clear, and the undertaking, mammoth as it was, in the long run caused as much confusion as clarification.[19]

Origen's broadened method of interpretation and his research are generally praised by most scholars of today. They see his new interpretations as having a "lasting, liberating influence" upon biblical studies.[20] Sadly, these scholars tend to ignore the realities of subsequent events. For, Origen's attempt to locate original sources was a step forward in scriptural studies, but in general his work produced a great step backward. The change of interpretation had the unfortunate result of encouraging a wide-ranging allegorical interpretation that eventually was used to discourage lay Bible reading. Consequently, in Origen's time grew the erroneous idea that only the learned could understand the scriptures. Eventually, because "allegory" came to be the major way to interpret the scriptures, church leaders felt that only they could understand them.[21] The movement in this direction was to become tragic.

By the fourth century A.D., many changes had occurred. On the one hand, outward appearances might indicate that the scriptures had triumphed. Under the influence of Constantine, the religious traditions of so-called Christianity and its holy scriptures seemed to prosper. In A.D. 332, the emperor Constantine ordered fifty sets of scripture made on vellum (animal skin), asking that they be "easy to read and conveniently portable" and stated as their purpose: "for the instruction of the church."[22]

But there are also clues that these open displays of success were deceiving and that many things were amiss. For one thing, education in general had declined in the third century, and Bible study had dwindled because church members found it boring. It wasn't that collections of scriptural writings weren't being made or sold; in fact, merchandising of scripture increased, and they even became popular sellers. But the purposes of possession had changed. The wealthy sought very fine and elegant copies—not to be read, but for display. In fact, some church leaders found it necessary to reprove the rich for not reading their expensive copies and to remind them that in comparison many of the poor showed more faithfulness by sharing and reading the few scriptures they'd been able to copy for themselves by hand.[23]

But in addition, for growing numbers of Christians, the biblical records began to take on an aura of abnormal sanctity, becoming objects of superstition and even being used as magic charms. The "lazy-minded found it easier to revere its pages than to try to understand them."[24]

The political upheavals of the fifth century, such as the invasions by the Goths and Vandals, also apparently contributed to declining scriptural usage. One fifth-century theologian in Antioch commented on the situation in his time: "Of other scriptures, most men know nothing. But the Psalms are repeated . . . by those who know them by heart, and feel the soothing power of their divine melodies."[25] For most persons, the Psalms alone became the scriptures.

By the fourth century precisely what was "official scripture" was finally decided. Athanasius (A.D. 293-373), the bishop of Alexandria, publicly listed as authoritative scripture the same twenty-seven books we have in our present New Testament. Some books whose authority scholars like Origen had ques-

tioned were included on this list—among them the books of
James, Hebrews, 2 Peter, and 2 and 3 John. Other books that
had been held dear by some early Christians were not on the
list, including the Epistle of Barnabas, the Didachê, 1 Clement,
the Apocalypse of Peter, and the Shepherd of Hermas.[26]

The list which Athanasius drew up was also accepted as
canonical (though not without debate), by the majority of those
church leaders present at the councils of Laodicea (A.D. 363),
Hippo (A.D. 393), and Carthage (A.D. 397). The last council,
after much disagreement on certain books, ratified as New Testament canon these same twenty-seven books and decreed that
none besides these should be read in the churches as divine
scripture.[27]

It should be pointed out that the questions of canonicity
taken up in these councils (in particular the councils at Hippo
and Carthage) pertained to Old Testament scriptures as well as
New. Some scriptures of the Old Testament period that were
not in the Hebrew Bible but were in the Greek Septuagint were
accepted as canon by these councils, although there had also
been prior disagreements about their respective worth. These
became the Apocrypha, which were reaffirmed by Catholicism
at the Council of Trent in 1546 and are still today a part of the
Catholic scriptural body.[28]

But in addition to these writings that were passed on as the
Apocrypha, there were others that were not passed on. In particular, apocalyptic or prophetic writings were those most often
cast aside—such works as the book of Enoch, for example. Dr.
Hugh Nibley points out the irony that these writings, which
had been rejected as canon by Pharisaic Judaism but accepted
as precious by the first Christians, were in time also rejected
by later Christians.[29] In recent years discoveries of ancient texts,
including the Dead Sea Scrolls, have reopened the questions of
what other writings were inspired and where the most accurate
texts might be.

Jerome and the Vulgate

Obviously, any message that is to be taken to the whole
world must go forth in the *languages* of the world. As we recall,

the first set of scriptures taken abroad was the Greek Septuagint, and when the New Testament scriptures began to multiply, for the most part they were also in the Greek language. But at length the need arose to take the scriptures into Latin-speaking areas, such as northern Africa; therefore, Latin translations were made. However, these translations were not closely controlled, and before long, church leaders became concerned about the many corruptions and variances in the separate texts.

To meet this problem, Pope Damasus in A.D. 384 commissioned his secretary, Jerome, a very able scholar in Greek and Latin, to produce an acceptable version. Jerome was extremly reluctant to undertake such a task, correctly anticipating that such a work would stir up bitter opposition. But because the pope himself had asked, he also hesitated to say no. In a response to this request, he expressed his inner turmoil:

> You have urged me to make a new work out of an old, and to sit in judgment, as it were, on the copies of the scriptures which are now scattered throughout the whole world; and, inasmuch as they differ from one another, you would have me decide which of them agree with the Greek original. This is a labor of piety, but at the same time one of dangerous presumption; for in judging others, I will myself be judged by all; and how dare I change the language of the world's old age and carry it back to the days of its childhood? Who is there, whether learned or unlearned, who, when he takes up the volume in his hands and discovers that what he reads therein does not agree with what he is accustomed to, will not break out at once in a loud voice and call me a sacrilegious forger, for daring to add something to the ancient books, to make changes and corrections in them?
>
> On the other hand, there are two considerations which console me: in the first place, the order comes from you, who are the supreme pontiff; secondly, even those who speak against us have to admit that divergent readings cannot [all] be right. For if we are to pin our faith to the Latin copies, our opponents must tell us *which*; for there are almost as many forms of texts *as* there are copies. If, on the other hand, we are to search out the truth by a comparison of many, why not go back to the original Greek and correct the mistakes intro-

duced either by inaccurate translators or by the blundering
emendations of self-confident but ignorant critics, or the additions and changes made by copyists who were only half-
awake?[30]

And so Jerome accepted the challenge. His initial work
was on the Psalms and the New Testament. As he himself
said in his work, he "restrained his pen," correcting only
passages that seemed to change the meaning from their
original intent and leaving the rest as they were.

The opposition that Jerome expected did arise, and indeed it pursued him most of his life. Unfortunately his pro-
tector, the pope, died the year the project began, but Jerome
continued the work anyway.

After his work on the New Testament was completed (a
labor of five years), Jerome journeyed to Bethlehem with the
intent of revising the Old Testament as well. He settled and
lived there the rest of his life. One of his purposes in going to
Bethlehem was to learn as much about Hebrew as he possibly
could to aid him in his translation. Because of the great antipathy
between Jew and Christian at that time, there was resentment
from both sides toward this purpose. Some elements among
the Jews felt that any assistance toward a Christian (and gentile)
Bible was traitorous, and there were already some restrictions
against Jews teaching Christians. Consequently, one of those
who taught him Hebrew dared not be seen with him by day
and visited him only in the dark of night.[31]

With the help of such Jews, Jerome continued to perfect his
Hebrew and to learn Aramaic and study Jewish traditions and
scriptural interpretations—all those things that he felt might be
helpful in producing the most correct Latin version of the Old
Testament. His work on the Old Testament was completed by
A.D. 405. It was a forceful translation that relied upon his understanding of the meaning or sense of the original rather than
upon the literal word-by-word translation.

From the Christian side, he was attacked fiercely by those
who felt he had betrayed Christianity by seeking knowledge
from the Jews and by going to the Hebrew Old Testament text
for help rather than relying solely on the Greek Septuagint,

which they considered of higher spiritual value. But Jerome argued (by letter and book) that Christianity's ignorance of Hebrew was an impediment to their understanding, bred prejudice, and was even dangerous as far as establishing correct theology. His advocacy of Hebrew studies to other Christians, however, was largely unsuccessful. He wrote of the fierceness of the attacks against himself: "I beg you to confront with the shields of your prayers the mad dogs who bark and rage against me and go about the city and in this think themselves learned if they disparage others."[32]

Jerome saw the value of his work in these terms, making reference to the ancient Israelite wilderness tabernacle, which was made both with fine and expensive materials as well as with common ones:

"I beg you, my reader, not to suppose that my labors are in any sense intended to disparage the ancient translators. For in the service of the tabernacle of God each one offers what he can: some gold and silver and precious stones, others linen and blue and scarlet; we shall do well if we offer skins and goat's hair. And yet the Apostle [Paul] pronounces our more contemptible parts the more necessary. Accordingly, the beauty of the whole tabernacle and of its various parts . . . was covered with skins and goats' hair cloths, and so the heat of the sun and the injurious rain were warded off by those things which were of less account."[33]

So Jerome felt that although his contribution to scriptural accuracy was inferior to the contributions of others, yet it was a necessary and helpful step as well.

By the end of his life, the opposition toward Jerome's work had abated somewhat. But it was a century or more before his Latin Old and New Testaments really replaced the Old Latin versions, and for many centuries thereafter strong minority voices were continually raised in opposition to its origins.

Nevertheless, Jerome's Bible in time supplanted all others, though there are those who contend that in its final victorious form his translation had become substantially corrupted by others. But pronounced authentic at the Council of Trent, the Vulgate, as Jerome's Latin Bible was known became *the* Bible of the Western world for a thousand years. One writer believes that it was the pillar which preserved Europe's spiritual and intellectual heritage against attacking waves of northern barbarism. He further points to it as the "source from which the Church has drawn the largest part of its ecclesiastical vocabulary. Terms now so familiar as to arouse no curiosity as to their origin, [such as] scripture, spirit, penance, sacrament, communion, salvation, propitiation, elements, grace, glory, conversion, discipline, sanctification, congregation, election, eternity, justification, all come from Jerome's Bible. It is an imperishable record of that commanding genius that could so manipulate and mould the majestic but inflexible language of Rome as to make it a fit and pliant instrument for the expression . . . of thought, of sentiments and images."[34]

But while the influence of Jerome's work would become longlasting, during the time of its supposed glory its influence was actually quite weak—because, for the most part, it was not read. Through the centuries that followed the translation of the Vulgate, many different forces contributed to a waning influence of the scriptures in the average Christian's life. While the reading of the scriptures had originally been a very central part of the earliest Christian services, scripture reading was replaced with ceremony. While private scripture study was energetically encouraged by the earliest Christian priesthood, in time it was actually discouraged. "The Bible was subordinated to the church itself as custodian of the truth."[35]

Substituted for the scriptures were legends about saints, and the church began to argue that since the true meaning of the scriptures was to be found in allegory, the scriptures were really too obscure for common members to comprehend. So the masses were to be kept from the "deep and obscure: and fed instead the simple and open, defined as the lives and deeds of the saints, the passions and triumphs of the martyrs, and other teaching concerning vices and virtues, . . . and the miseries of the damned."[36] Obviously, there was little scriptural content in such teachings.

Furthermore, the language of the Bible—Latin—and the everchanging languages of the people became divergent; nor was there much effort to make copies of the Bible available to the people themselves. In a sense, the uniting of the Old and the New Testaments contributed to the Bible's lack of availability. Before, certain portions might be obtained as separate parchments or scrolls. But the full Latin Bible, copied by hand by monks in monasteries, could not be contained even in one volume. In spite of using a writing style that ran all the letters together and included some shorthand (for example: "THEBE-GINNINGOTHGOSPELOJESUSXTHESONOGOD"), the space required for handwriting and the greater thickness of vellum increased the bulk of these copies of the Bible to two and sometimes four volumes. Such copies were rare, expensive, and very cumbersome.

The effort required to produce copies of the Bible was also enormous. The labor and discomfort of those who served as copyists have been found in various writings of the period. One scribe wrote, "I am very cold"; and still another wrote, "while the fingers write, the back is bent, the ribs sink into the stomach, and the whole body suffers."[37]

Thus there was little motivation to produce Bibles for the masses. Those made were elaborate, with covers and cover pages beautifully ornamented and gilded, and with painstaking embellishments in the copy. The effect of such labor was to make the scriptures "treasures of art" but not of knowledge.

In a sense, then, the Bible became a holy relic. It was not meant to be read or studied, for even monks came to regard its contents as "sacrosanct but ill-understood lore, a venerable mystery."[38] Its contents were no longer penetrated by eager minds, nor memorized, nor treasured by softened hearts. In general, it became an unopened enigma, only to be kissed and superstitiously revered.

CHAPTER FIVE

Glimmers of Light in Darkness

It is interesting that the darkness of the Middle Ages lasted about as long as the Millenium's light will last—a thousand years. The Middle Ages began in the mid-fifth century A.D. with the fall of the Western Empire and lasted until the mid-fifteenth century, when several momentous events, including the Renaissance, the Reformation, and the invention of the printing press, brought these darker ages to an end and prepared the way for the Restoration.

Though the Middle Ages are noted more for retrogression than for progress, there were exceptions. Among the exceptions was a continuation of the spread of the Christian religion to distant lands, including Britain, which came to play a significant part in future struggles to make the scriptures available in the language of common men.

There is evidence that Christianity had reached England's shores in the second century,[1] but events such as invasions by the Teutons had stifled its flames. In the sixth century, however, St. Augustine, first Archbishop of Canterbury, and others were sent to Britain to preach. Behind them came other missionaries. Bede's *Ecclesiastical History* reports that Theodore of Tarsus, who was well read in the scriptures, came as a missionary about A.D. 700. He and his companion gathered the people and poured forth "rivers of knowledge to water the hearts of their hearers,"[2] teaching them both scriptural and secular knowledge. One of the most important things they did was to teach people how to read the scriptures. The scriptures, of course, were in Latin. Usually those who chose to learn were those who became a part of the English clergy.

Through succeeding years, the majority of Britons were nurtured on Bible stories and principles of discipline and conduct. There was no real study of the scriptures. Worship, as elsewhere, was effected through ceremony, and in Latin. To remind the people of the Bible's stories, biblical scenes were painted on church walls and carved into panels. Later, elaborate religious plays were devised.[3]

The lack of education on the part of the masses and the very limited availability of scriptures were enormous obstacles to significant scriptural understanding. There were, however, a few good shepherds who had sincere desires to feed the sheep with food they could truly digest.

One of the first steps toward translating the scriptures into a language the people could understand was made by a simple herdsman named Caedmon. According to Bede, Caedmon had a special gift for composing Anglo-Saxon verse based on the scriptures. His gift was so unusual that he was taken into a monastery where he learned scriptures and then turned them into verse, making "his masters in their turn his hearers." Before the lowly and the powerful he sang the record of the Jews — about "the creation of the world, the origin of man, and all the history of Genesis." He sang the history of the children of Israel and the life and mission of the Lord.[4] The value of his work was that he provided a people's Bible that they could easily memorize and sing themselves.

Another who took the Christian religion to the common people in their own tongue was Aldhelm, Abbot of Malmesbury. During and after mass, which was in Latin and therefore undiscernible to the people, he would stand upon a bridge and, disguised as a wandering minstrel, sing songs which contained much scripture.[5]

During the seventh, eighth, and ninth centuries, several written Anglo-Saxon translations of parts of the scriptures existed, usually the Psalms and the Gospels. But the common people generally had little access to these translations, although some of the clergy did continue to encourage more scriptural knowledge in the laity. The great scholar and clergyman Bede (A.D. 673-735) himself took some steps in this direction. In a letter to Bishop Egbert he wrote, "But make the unlearned . . . learn [some scriptural passages] in their own language, and carefully repeat them; and this should be done, not only in the case of laymen . . . but also in the case of monks and clerks, who know Latin."[6]

In spite of such efforts, continual political upheavals prevented literacy in the scriptures from gaining much ground. When Alfred became king in 871 following a period of great upheaval, he lamented that although there had been some kinds of progress, there had also been great setbacks:

"I remembered also how I saw, before it had all been ravaged and burnt, how the churches throughout the whole of England stood filled with treasures and books, and there was also a great multitude of God's servants, but they had very little knowledge of the books, for they could not understand anything of them, because they were no't written in their own language."[7]

Alfred was himself an educated man, unusual in those days for kings. Obviously he was much dismayed at the waste of books that could not be read because of destruction and ignorance, so he set out to make changes. He himself translated and commissioned the translation of many books, including portions of the scriptures. And in establishing the laws that would govern his people, he began with a translated version of the Ten Commandments, to which he added the golden rule.

Limited as it was, Alfred's use of the scriptures and his desire to educate his people resulted in a remarkable flowering of civilization. One historian observes:

"At the middle of the seventh century there was nothing to suggest the imminence of a great English achievement in learning and literature. The strongest of English kings was an obdurate heathen [probably Penda, ca. 632-654]. The country was distracted by wars, which destroyed the peace of scholars. . . . The Christian faith, which was to carry imagination into new worlds, was only secure in the extreme south-east of the island. *Within a hundred years England had become the home of a Christian culture which influenced the whole development of letters and learning in western Europe.* . . . There is nothing in European history closely parallel to this sudden development of a civilization by one of the most primitive people established within the ancient Roman empire."[8]

After King Alfred's death, there were a few additional steps toward making scriptures more usable. "Interlinear glosses," literal translations into Anglo-Saxon written between the lines of the Latin Bibles, were made—but these were quite rare. A greater step was taken toward the end of the tenth century when Aelfric, the Archbishop of Canterbury, translated several Old Testament books into Anglo-Saxon. A little light had glimmered in the darkness.

Then the Normans conquered England. French became the language of the ruling classes, and though parts of the Bible were translated into French for use by some of the Norman rulers, little was done to make the scriptures available to the Anglo-Saxons. Further attempts to translate the Bible into the language of the common man had to wait another three hundred years.

The spread of Christianity to lands such as England proved in time to be one of the greatest challenges to the Roman church. The Greek church had continued its belief that knowledge was essential to salvation; therefore, when peoples of other cultures were converted, translations were made into their language—such as Russian and Bulgarian. The Roman church, on the other hand, did not encourage vernacular translations, even though the Latin Vulgate had itself been a translation into a language spoken by the people—before time and changing language had turned it into a "sacred language" used only in church services.

In fact, during the time of Pope Gregory VII (A.D. 1073-85) a policy *against* translations took shape. In a struggle with the Greek church for influence in certain disputed territories, Gregory saw that promoting reliance upon Latin in these areas was to the Roman church's political advantage. He also decided that it would be advantageous to create a sharper distinction between laity and clergy. The clergy thus became the *teachers* of the church, while the laity became *receivers* only. "From [Pope Gregory's] time onwards," asserts one scholar, "orthodox prejudice against lay knowledge of the Biblical text hardened." [9]

Consequently, the stage was set for one of the greatest dramas in the history of man — the struggle over vernacular translations between a few courageous individuals and the Inquisition that swept Europe during the last centuries of the Middle Ages. In the earliest battles, the weight of advantage went definitely to the Inquisition.

Sometime during the 1170s in southern France, one of the first skirmishes of this battle was enacted. According to one account, it began this way: "A certain rich man of the city [Lyons], called Waldo, was curious when he heard the gospel read [in Latin] since he was not much lettered, to know what was said. Wherefore he made a pact with certain priests, the one that he should translate to him the Bible: the other, that he should write as the first dictated. Which they did; and in like manner many books of the Bible . . . which when the said citizen had often read and learned by heart, he . . . sold all his goods, and despising the world, he gave all his money to the poor, and usurped the apostolic office by preaching the gospel, and those things which he had learned by heart. [10]

Waldo's "preaching" among the people consisted mostly of reciting passages from the scriptures in the common tongue. Evidently he did not set out with the intent to oppose the church, but merely to enlighten the people. An eyewitness at the Lateran Council of 1179 wrote of Waldo's initial attempts to get church approval for his activities — and of the church's negative reaction: "We saw the Waldensians [supporters of Waldo] at the council celebrated at Rome under pope Alexander III. They were simple and illiterate men . . . and they presented to the lord pope a book written in the French tongue, in which were contained a text and gloss on the psalter, and on very many other books of both testaments. These besought with great urgency that authority to preach should be confirmed to them, for they thought themselves expert, when they were scarcely learned at all." [11]

The writer then voices feelings that became entrenched as argument against giving scriptures to the common man: "In every small point of the sacred page, so many meanings fly on the wings of virtue, such stores of wealth are accumulated, that only he can fully exhaust them whom God has inspired. Shall not therefore the Word given to the unlearned be as *pearls before swine*, when we know them to be fitted neither to receive it, nor to give out what they have received? Away with this idea, and let it be rooted out. *The ointment ran down from the head, even to the skirts of his clothing:* waters flow from the spring, not from the mud of public ways."[12]

But the Waldensians were not easily dissuaded from seeking scriptural knowledge. Like their peers, they were not "lettered," nor had they access to many copies of scripture, but they overcame this obstacle by *memorizing* surprising lengths of scripture when they were given the opportunity.

The Waldensians suffered because of their desire for knowledge. They were tried by the Inquisition, excommunicated, imprisoned, and burned as heretics. Their books were banned — and when found, burned. At their trials and in the tracts written against them, their great "crime" as stated was that they "translated the New and Old Testament into the vulgar tongue and this they teach and learn. For I have heard and seen a certain unlettered countryman who used to recite Job word for word, and many others who knew the whole New Testament perfectly."[13]

"All men and women, cease not to teach and learn, night and day. The workman, who toils by day, learns or teaches at night. . . . They teach and learn without books . . . and even in leper-houses. . . . To those who excuse themselves, saying that they cannot learn, they say; 'learn only one word a day, and in a year's time you will learn three hundred, and thus you will grow proficient.'"[14]

In spite of attempts to stifle it, the Waldensian movement, and others similar to it, spread into neighboring Italy and Spain. And upon their heels followed official pronouncements against their work — banning the preaching, reading, memorizing, *or even possessing* of scriptures.[15] Penalties for disobedience were extremely severe. According to one inquisitor general's record in an area near Toulouse, France, 930 sentences against heretics were pronounced during a period of fifteen years, and 114 heretics were destroyed by flames.[16]

But even as the Inquisition tried to stamp out the Waldensian movement in France, Italy, and Spain, the hunger for scripture cropped up elsewhere, this time in England and Germany. The movement in England began in the mid-1300s. Unlike the Waldensian movement, which was begun by those totally outside the church's power structure (though some clergy later joined it), the English movement was spearheaded by one of the most prominent and respected scholars and clergymen of his age — John Wycliffe.

The Wycliffe Translation

Wycliffe is described as being frail in physical stature, but intellectually and spiritually he was a giant. He was the most prominent scholar at the most prestigious school of his day, Oxford, but his scholarship was unique for that time because it included a thorough knowledge and appreciation of the scriptures, earning for him a special title, "the evangelical doctor." While his colleagues viewed the Bible as a "treasure-house of dead dogma,"[17] Wycliffe grew to love it and drew his strength from it — and in later controversy, pled to be judged by its standards.

It was partly the social conditions of England in Wycliffe's day that aroused him, for there was much amiss. The priests who were closest to the people were themselves ignorant, but the clergymen who had education lived in luxury and were insensitive to the wretched state in which the peasants lived. Often, those supposedly called to be exemplars of Christ sought and maintained their positions of power through corruption and bribery and were frequently guilty of other vices. There were incessant power struggles between arms of the church and between church and state.[18]

Wycliffe was troubled by what he saw, and his "inmost soul was stirred to its depth by the spectacle of social wretchedness which was rife."[19] But the catalyst that drove him to action was the papal schism of 1378. Because of his study of the Bible, Wycliffe felt confident that his religious convictions were consistent with the principles taught by the prophets and apostles. He understood that the true standard for the church must be meekness, not worldliness; and when he saw two opposing popes fighting for status and power he could not withhold his dismay.[20]

Disillusioned with the contemporary church and feeling that its actions were inconsistent with the teachings of the Bible, Wycliffe came to the conclusion that the only just guide that the people still had was the Bible. It was "God's Law," and he felt that under present conditions men should be held accountable to it alone.[21] The people, however, could not be held accountable for a law they did not know. The goal of his life, then, became taking "Goddis Lawe" to the people in the language they understood, which was English.

Wycliffe drew other men to help him in this work. Many were responsive to his lead because of his scholastic reputation and his high character. He organized them to be preachers and to take the scriptures to the people — not to churches but to the common people in their streets, in their homes, in their fields, in their shops. There, in friendly conversation, they sought to read the scriptures to the people. They carried sheets of the New Testament that had been translated into Middle English, the language of that day.

The work of keeping the preachers supplied with scriptures was not easy. After being translated from the Latin, each sheet of scripture had to be copied by hand. Explanatory sheets were also handwritten so that the preachers could explain the scriptures while reading them.

The preachers sent out by Wycliffe actually held no official license to preach. Known as *Lollards*, they were students or clerks who did this work during their vacations. They seemed suddenly to spring up everywhere. "You cannot travel anywhere in England but of every two men you meet one will be a Lollard," one man wrote.[22]

The work of Wycliffe and his Lollards certainly was not unopposed. But Wycliffe had not assumed it would be. In 1379 he published a treatise entitled *On the Truth of Holy Scripture*, in which he admitted that he expected to be silenced eventually through some punitive form of death. In that regard he was wrong. He did not suffer death for his actions, probably because of his prominent position, his politically powerful friends, and the weakened condition of the papacy.[23] Yet he did suffer. There were attempts to put him on trial, though they failed. He was publicly attacked from the most prestigious pulpits, was the subject of furious controversy in the schools, and finally was removed from his position at Oxford. He was severely isolated from any outwardly respectable role in society.

Deserted by all but the most faithful of his friends and followers, he nevertheless remained steadfastly anchored in his belief that in time truth would prevail. Perhaps, in a way, his forced retirement was a blessing, for it enabled him to complete his greatest work — the translation of the entire Bible into the language of the people.

As we have seen, there were several earlier translations of portions of the Bible; but to Wycliffe goes the honor for the first complete translation from Latin into English. Such a work, particularly in those days, was a tremendous undertaking. It isn't clear how much of the work Wycliffe actually did himself and how many assistants he had, but there is evidence that he had the assistance of at least two others — Nicholas de Hereford, a Lollard leader, and John Purvey, Wycliffe's talented secretary.[24]

The previous partial translations made in Britain were of little help in their work. According to Purvey, they were in "so olde Englische that unnethe [hardly] can any man rede them."[25] And so, before Wycliffe and the others began the work of translating from the Latin, they made careful studies of many copies of the Latin, searching for the oldest and most reliable. In this, Wycliffe was most fortunate. Although England had taken an early lead in turning portions of the scriptures into its native tongue, it had also been a leader in its devotion to the Latin Bible. One writer shows that the most reliable existing ancient manuscripts of the Latin Vulgate were copied and preserved in England.[26]

Wycliffe and his assistants also studied commentaries and writings of biblical scholars so that they could begin on the surest footing. And then they made as near a literal word-for-word translation as possible, even keeping the order of the words the same as they would be in Latin, though the natural English order was different.

The text of this translation contains clues of tragic drama. The original Old Testament version, for instance, ends abruptly in the middle of Baruch 3:20 with this note: "Here ends the translation of Nicholas of Hereford." Evidence suggests that the abrupt cessation of his work was due to his arrest; he and others were tried and excommunicated at Canterbury, and he spent the following five years in prison or on the continent.[27]

In spite of the persecution, the work on the Bible continued, and the New Testament was finally completed, followed by the Old. The work appeared in parcels rather than in one volume.

Wycliffe died soon after the completion of the entire work. "Towards the close of the year (1382) the mental strain, under which he had long gone on working with all his indefatigable industry and courage, brought on a stroke of paralysis. Two years later came the end. While celebrating mass in Lutterworth Church he was struck for the second time, and the 31st of December he died."[28]

Perhaps it is well that Wycliffe died so shortly after the translation was done. Because of its strong popularity among the people (and because knowledge of the Bible tended to increase dissatisfaction with the church), the translation soon stirred the fears and hatred of many people. An epitaph written at St. Albans called Wycliffe "the devil's instrument, church's enemy, people's confusion, heretic's idol, hypocrite's mirror, schism's broacher, hatred's sower, lies' forger, flatteries' sink, who, stricken by the horrible judgment of God, breathed forth his soul to the dark mansion of the black devil."[29] The animosity toward Wycliffe grew to such a state that years later his body was ordered dug up, his bones destroyed by fire, and his ashes cast into the river.[30]

With the death of Wycliffe and the distribution of manuscripts of his Bible, the safety of those who had associated with him was greatly jeopardized. They were hunted, excommunicated, imprisoned, tortured, and burned. Yet somehow, during the early years of this persecution, Purvey and Hereford and others were able to complete in 1388 a second version of the translated Bible.

Recognizing that the Latin-based form of the first version made it too difficult for the common man to read, they put their second version in a form much more compatible with the English usage of that day. Purvey, who led the project, explains their reasons for seeking to improve the translation: "First, it is to be known that the best translating out of the Latin into English is to translate after the sentence and not only after the words, so that the sentence be as open, or opener [easy to understand] in English as in Latin, and go not far from the letter; and if the letter may not be followed in the translating, let the sentence ever be whole and open, for the words ought to serve to the intent and sentence, or else the words be superfluous or false."[31]

Purvey was not unmindful of the great responsibilities his group bore in attempting to translate holy scripture. He took this work very seriously: "A translator hath great need to study well the sense both before and after, and then also he hath need to live a clean life and be full devout in prayers, and have not his wit occupied about worldly things, that the Holy Spirit, author of all wisdom and knowledge and truth, dress him for his work and suffer him not to err. By this manner, with good living and great travail, men can come to true and clear translating, and true understanding of holy writ, seem it ever so hard at the beginning."[32]

Like the first version, this second version of Wycliffe's Bible appeared anonymously, for obvious reasons, though the authorities probably had little doubt about who was behind it. Purvey had been correct in asserting that "the unlearned cry after Holy Writ to know it, with great cost and peril to their lives,"[33] for people did indeed risk their liberties, their properties, and their lives to have as much as they could of this Bible, even if it were to possess or to hear just a few pages. In 1414 a law was established that would cause those who read any scriptures in English to "forfeit land, catel, lif[e], and goods from their heyers [heirs] for ever."[34] The church was in earnest, and there were many prosecutions. One woman was accused of heresy simply for listening in the secret of the night to her husband read the words of Christ. Others suffered for memorizing the Bible's passages, regardless of the content. Another woman was tried for teaching someone else "the Epistle of James, the first chapter of Luke, and the Sermon on the Mount." She was strictly instructed to teach the Bible no more, especially to her children.[35] Many men and women who were convicted were burned at the stake, often with their Bibles hung around their necks.

The principals of the movement were spared death but suffered imprisonment, evidently experiencing such horrors while in prison that they finally recanted, Purvey being the last to do so in 1401. It was recognized, however, even by the authorities, that his recantation was not sincere, and he was kept thereafter under close surveillance. As much as he dared, he continued to defend the need for English Bibles.

In spite of burnings, recantations, and severe penalties, the people's hunger for the word of God was too great to squelch. The Wycliffe Bibles continued to circulate surreptitiously, and a surprising number of manuscripts (over 150) have been preserved even to modern times. One method evidently used to preserve them from harm was to disguise them: in some of these manuscripts, the date of writing was deliberately changed (manuscripts written before certain laws were passed were not subject to those laws); others were falsely ascribed to other translators.[36]

The manuscripts, even detached sheets, were so valuable to the common man that they elicited sums that would surprise modern readers. It is reported that a whole load of hay (imagine the labor involved in those days in raising and harvesting a load of hay) was given in exchange for just a few chapters of St. James or St. Paul. One historian, writing in 1956, figured the cost for an entire Wycliffe Bible as equal to $150.00 in Wycliffe's day.[37]

Records show that trials for those accused of reading Wycliffe's Bible continued throughout the 1400s. Even as late as 1496 there is record of five Lollards being burned at Paul's Cross, "with the books of their lore hanging around them, which books were at the time of the sermon there burnt."[38]

But as there is tragedy, so there is irony in this story. Because many of the Wycliffe Bibles were written without any indication whatsoever that they originated from Wycliffe and the Lollards, these sometimes came into the possession of influential orthodox members of the church. Although the official church position was that Wycliffe's work itself was of the devil, no action was taken against these individuals for possessing it. In fact, it is claimed by some that when the first Elizabeth assumed the throne in 1558, *The work of Truth* publicly presented to her at that time was actually the hated Wycliffe Bible, still officially banned.[39]

The church obviously felt justified in what seems to us a very unjust discrimination. The roots of this discrimination rest in several factors. First, the belief continued that most of the Bible was allegorical and that the common man could not comprehend it without an interpreter. As one fifteenth-century scholar said, "It is dangerous to put knives into children's hands for them to cut bread with themselves, for they may cut themselves. So also holy scripture, which contains the bread of God."[40]

Part of this discrimination also was due to a poor opinion of the commoner. Pope Gregory VII had written: "It is clear to those who reflect upon it, that not without reason has it pleased Almighty God that holy scriptures should be a secret in certain places, lest, if it were plainly apparent to all men, perchance it would be little esteemed and be subject to disrespect; or it might be falsely understood by those of mediocre learning, and lead to error."[41] As another writer put it, "It was one thing for a King to have the Bible in French, or for English nuns to read the Psalms in English under the direction of their confessor; but it was quite another thing when 'the very cooks who sod the pottage made good their claim to read the Bible in Wycliffe's English.'"[42]

The church claimed the right to interpret the scriptures to the masses. But, having generally abandoned the scriptures as a basis of the faith, the church did not fulfill that duty. All church service was in ceremonial Latin, which few of the parish priests themselves understood. Nor did they understand any better their Latin Bibles.[43] Consequently, the clergy could not feed the sheep, for they had no knowledge with which to feed them.

Other Translations

There were some exceptions, however, in Germany. In the thirteenth century the Waldensian movement had significant influence there; and in the following centuries, in spite of conflicts over translating the scriptures into native tongues, support for vernacular translations existed among some German clergy.

Generally this support came from groups such as the Friends of God who endeavored to educate interested laity. Such work naturally led to a desire to make some scripture knowledge available to them. But because these clergymen desired that many books of edification be translated, not just the Bible — and then only the "understandable" parts of the Bible — their translation did not become the lightning rod for controversy that the English translations became. Furthermore, at Cologne in 1398, a group of university scholars were called upon, because of the Inquisition, to give their opinions on vernacular translations. They concluded that translations could not logically be forbidden. Citing the number of languages into which the scriptures already existed — Latin, Hebrew, Chaldean, Gothic, Egyptian, etc. — they argued, "What then is the reason that holy scripture may be read in the tongues of so many nations, yet not in the German language?"[44]

In 1430 another language was added to that list: a Spanish translation was made, though not for the common people. And in 1466 a German Bible finally emerged, probably a composite of previously translated portions. Its preface included the following words:

> This is a foreword against him, who is opposed to the German writing, which is, nevertheless, useful and profitable for men's souls, My enemies have up till now done violence to their own conscience, because they have till now been silent as regards my plan to translate the holy gospel into German. Now however they have taken a different stand, inspired by foolish pride, and they bring forward foolish counsels, and say: "But what shall we now preach, when men read and listen to the holy scriptures in the German tongue in their rooms and houses?"
>
> Him will I answer from holy scripture. . . . Woe to you who call good evil, and evil good: . . . and fight against the righteous truth: that is, they fight against the holy scriptures and hinder the spread of their revealing.[45]

Although in Germany there were some orthodox leanings toward translations, the largest concentration of power was strongly opposed to it, especially as a book for common usage. There were those in Germany who suffered death for possessing Bibles, particularly the Beghards, who were considered heretical. After 1509 a few orthodox groups in Germany evidently allowed limited study of parts of the translated Bible by members of the laity. But they were the exception. The many everywhere were denied.[46]

The weight of advantage in this great struggle may have remained in favor of those who opposed translation for centuries more, but in the fifteenth century came a remarkable event that shifted the advantage to the people — the invention of the printing press. Even then the struggle for vernacular translations was far from over yet. Many individuals would still give their lives for its cause. But light had come out of darkness, and with it the hunger for more light.

And light is the essence of all good beginnings, as Wycliffe had revealed to the people through his beloved English Bible:

> *In the first made God of nought heaven and earth.*[47]
> *The earth, forsooth, was vain within and void.*
> *And darknessis weren upon the face of the see.*
> *And the spirit of God was born upon the waters.*
> *And God said, Be made light*
> *And made is light.*
> *And God saw light that it was good.*[48]

CHAPTER SIX

No Price Too Great

By the 1500s the darkness of the Middle Ages was drawing to a close. New discoveries were illuminating every field of learning, and a spirit of new life permeated society. It was the time of the Renaissance. Two events of that time would have an especially telling influence on the years ahead. The first was Johann Gutenberg's invention of the printing press sometime during the 1430s.

Gutenberg's invention required an enormous sacrifice from him, demanding vast amounts of time and his personal indebtedness. He died without realizing much return on his investment; but, like so many other major sacrifices, the result would be a blessing to others, not the least of which would be making the Bible more readily available. Indeed, when he realized he had mastered the technique of printing, he sensed his first responsibility was to print the Bible, and a printed Latin Bible was the first major work to come from this remarkable new invention. The development of printing and the work on the Bible together absorbed over twenty years of Gutenberg's life.[1]

The second event to influence the dissemination of the Bible was the fall of Constantinople to the Turks in 1453. This caused a major reorientation of the scholastic centers of Europe, attracting to the Roman church and its areas of influence new pioneers of thought and study from the East. A great movement to return to the very origins of knowledge arose; and among those works whose foundations were sought was the Bible.[2]

Such developments, joined with the courage of men willing to sacrifice for a righteous cause, were the forces that at last paved the way toward putting the holy scriptures into the hands of the common people.

Among those who gave impetus to the movement for a people's Bible was a Dutchman best known by his Greek name: Erasmus. In the early 1500s, with a newly obtained knowledge of Greek, Erasmus spent several years teaching at Cambridge as a professor of Greek and Divinity. His Greek studies had spurred in him a desire to produce a New Testament as close to its original Greek form as possible, and from it a better Latin version. Both were revolutionary undertakings in that day; for Jerome's work, although once bitterly attacked, was now considered sacrosanct and untouchable.[3]

But Erasmus argued that corruption through the years had crept into the Vulgate. "How is it that Jerome, Augustine, and Ambrose all cite a text which differs from the Vulgate? . . . Will you, treating all this with contempt, follow a version corrupted by some copyist? . . . In doing so you follow in the steps of those vulgar divines who are accustomed to attribute ecclesiastical authority to whatever in anyway creeps into general use."[4]

While Erasmus worked on his Greek New Testament, a Spanish Cardinal, Ximines, labored over one containing Hebrew, Greek, and Latin translations. The Cardinal would actually complete his work before Erasmus, but because of opposition from the Inquisition, Erasmus's work was first to be published.[5] Both had the benefit of the new printing techniques, and both would affect later translations of the Bible.

While Erasmus and Ximines experienced bitter opposition, there is no evidence that their lives were seriously endangered. Both were loyal to the authority of the church, seeking reforms from within it rather than outside it.[6] Furthermore, the translations both made were in languages in which the scriptures already existed, and were accomplished solely for scholarly purposes.

Yet Erasmus's work led him to value the right of the people

to use the scriptures. "I totally disagree," he wrote, "with those who are unwilling that the sacred scriptures, translated into the vulgar tongue, should be read by private individuals, as if Christ had taught such subtle doctrines that they can with difficulty be understood by a very few theologians, or as if the strength of the Christian religion lay in men's ignorance of it. . . .

"I wish that even the weakest woman should read the Gospel. . . . And I wish these were translated into all languages, so that they might be read and understood. . . . I long that the husbandman should sing portions of them to himself as he follows the plough, and that the weaver should hum them to the tune of his shuttle."[7]

Although Erasmus had uttered the longing cry, it remained for another, William Tyndale, to fulfill that longing.

The Tyndale Translation

It is generally agreed that William Tyndale was born in the early 1490s, around the same time as Columbus's discovery of America. At the age of twelve or thirteen, Tyndale went to Oxford, then to Cambridge for additional schooling. Although he arrived in Cambridge after Erasmus had left, he undoubtedly fell under the lingering influence of Erasmus's teachings and writings.[8] Even so, the great influence on Tyndale was of a more primal origin. "William Tyndale was . . . [learned] especially in the knowledge of the Scriptures, whereunto his mind was singularly addicted, [and he] read privily to certain students and fellows . . . instructing them in their knowledge and truth."[9]

Fresh from his university education, Tyndale accepted a position in Sodbury as chaplain or tutor to the prominent Walsh family. It was a comfortable position that permitted him time for study, but his discontent grew as he perceived a great ignorance on scriptural matters among many of the clergy as well as the laity, and he found it difficult to keep his peace. Eventually, his continued disputations with others because they lacked knowledge of what the scriptures said brought him before local ecclesiastical authority, where he was harshly scolded for his views.[10]

No one knows precisely when Tyndale decided on his life's

course, but at one point, during an encounter with a learned
gentleman, Tyndale was provoked to exclaim that if God would
spare his life, before many years the boy who guided the plough
would know more scriptures than those who were supposedly
learned.[11]

And so Tyndale embarked on a mission to open the scriptures to the people. Like so many before him, he nurtured a
hope that his work could be done with the church's blessing.
This was difficult, however, because there were powerful laws
against vernacular translations unless previously approved by
a bishop. Since Erasmus had written highly of Tunstal, bishop
of London, as one who supported the new learning, Tyndale
hoped to obtain a position with Tunstal and his support for the
work. To help pave the way, Tyndale took with him a letter of
introduction and samples of his translative skills. Tunstal's dis-
appointing and abrupt reply was that he had no room in his
house for him, that he should seek employment elsewhere.[12]

Still, Tyndale's trip to London was not without success.
While waiting for his interview with Tunstal, he preached a few
times at a local church. There he impressed a wealthy merchant
named Monmouth, who befriended him and, after Tyndale's
rejection by Tunstal, made a place for him in his household.
Tyndale remained there for six months, quietly working, obtain-
ing information and making useful acquaintances among Monmouth's business associates, who brought back news from the
Continent about Luther's work there and of the printing
capabilities in Germany. Fortified by these reports and supported by his new friends, in the spring of 1524 Tyndale sailed
for Germany. He would never return.

Tyndale's life abroad has been difficult to trace because he
felt it necessary at times to travel and live under assumed names,
but it is now believed he traveled first to Wittenberg, where
Luther resided, possibly because Luther had already made a
vernacular translation of the New Testament into German.[13]
The spread of Lutheranism in Europe had moved the Roman
church to constant watchfulness and strong action, so Tyndale
found it wise to work in secret and several times to quietly
disappear for safety's sake. Indeed, after a year in Wittenberg,
growing danger forced him to move to Hamburg.[14]

We know little of the difficulties Tyndale faced in preparing his manuscript for printing, but we would be mistaken if we assumed it came easily. Luther, relating the struggles in making his translation, observed: "Sometimes for three and four weeks we have sought and asked for a single word and sometimes we have not found it even then. In working at the book of Job, [my associates] and I could sometimes scarcely finish three lines in four days."[15] Tyndale, working alone, surely did not find translating any easier. For obvious reasons, the printing had to be done in secret.

However difficult the work had been, by August 1525 Tyndale was in Cologne, a city well known for its printing presses, with a nearly completed manuscript. Unfortunately, the printers were not always circumspect. One commented to a friend that a certain work they were printing would make all of England Lutheran. The remark was noted by a man with strong Roman sentiments who, through trickery, obtained from the printers a description of the work. This information was relayed to authorities in Cologne and England, and the Cologne authorities immediately prevented further printing of the book.[16]

Tyndale again fled, taking the printed sheets with him. His destination this time was Worms, where Lutheran sympathies were much stronger and the printing safer. Knowing that the English authorities had been forewarned and thus expected his work, Tyndale tried to outmanuever them by printing two editions, neither of which would bear his name nor the correct names and places of the printing houses.

The first edition off the presses was a translation of the New Testament in English. It carried a simple, unsigned postscript begging the readers to come to the scriptures with pure minds and with eyes single to the truth, that they might harvest spiritual blessings. Tyndale further pleaded that they not be overly critical of defects, for it was his first attempt at translating the sacred books. Not yet totally satisfied with his rendering, he vowed that if God would permit, he would in the future perfect this initial offering. "Count it as a thing not having his full shape, but as it were born before his time, even as a thing begun rather than finished."[17]

Once the printing was completed, the help of the merchants

Tyndale had met in England became particularly valuable. English authorities were on the alert, and strict instructions had been given to prevent Tyndale's New Testament from entering England. But the testaments entered anyway — six thousand copies of them, hidden under bales of innocent-appearing imported goods. There were many eager hands waiting to receive them.[18]

Having failed in keeping the books from being printed and from entering England, the church took strong measures to at least prevent them from being read. To demonstrate their opposition, church authorities built a bonfire where they publicly burned any books they found. Tunstal and others, including Sir Thomas More, publicly attacked the accuracy of the translation itself, claiming it contained thousands of errors.[19] Tunstal also ordered that anyone coming into possession of these New Testaments must relinquish them for burning or face excommunication. The authorities felt their actions justified, insisting that "No burnt offering could be better pleasing to God."[20]

Tyndale later commented that "in burning the New Testament, they did none other thing than I looked for; no more shall they do if they burn me also, if it be God's will it shall so be."[21] Out of an estimated 18,000 copies printed between 1524 and 1528, fewer than a handful of copies have survived to modern times.[22] And yet, ironically, the burning actually helped provide resources for more printing. The story is told that Tunstal decided the policy of burning books would be more effective if the books could be confiscated before they reached England. While on a visit to Antwerp, he approached a merchant named Packington and expressed his desires to obtain and burn English translations of the New Testament because of their errors and evil influence. He offered Packington considerable money to buy all he could. Packington agreed to the bargain; but, sympathetic to Tyndale, he went immediately to him and described what Tunstal was doing: "William, I know thou art a poor man, and hast a heap of New Testaments and books by thee, for the which thou hast both endangered thy friends and beggared thyself; and I have now gotten thee a merchant, which with ready money shall dispatch thee of all that thou hast."[23]

Tyndale was quite pleased. He saw two advantages in such

a bargain: the money paid would get him out of debt and provide the resources to continue his work, and the public burning of scriptures would outrage the public. The bargain was accepted.[24]

Sometime later Sir Thomas More, strongly anti-Protestant, interrogated another merchant accused of heresy. More also offered a bargain: he would show the heretic mercy in the accusation if the merchant would reveal but one thing—who was giving financial support to Tyndale and his associates? "'Truly,' quoth he, 'it is the bishop of London that hath holpen us; for he hath bestowed among us a great deal of money in New Testaments to burn them, and that hath been, and yet is, our only succour and comfort.'"[25]

Much of the money that Tunstal had paid to purchase the Bibles for burning had been raised by him from other clergymen. Thus, he unwittingly became Tyndale's biggest single source of financial assistance. But the books also sold well on their own, in spite of the warnings and the burnings, in spite of arrests and imprisonments of sellers and buyers. Despite the fact that the cost of a New Testament was as much as a full week's pay for a skilled laborer, the books were bought, secreted, and read. So good was the market for them, in fact, that enterprising businessmen in Holland printed copies of their own and sought to undersell those from Germany.[26]

The authorities continued to try to stem the tide, continually attacking the quality of Tyndale's work. Commissioned by Tunstal, Sir Thomas More began a six-year series of publications that would amount to over a thousand pages against Tyndale, his work, and his motivation. He said that searching for errors in the translation was like searching for water in the sea.[27]

As we shall see, however, time would prove Tyndale's translation basically very good. Tyndale himself complained that if there was even so much as an *i* undotted, someone would call it heresy. He also insisted, "I never altered one syllable of God's words against my conscience; nor would do this day, if all that is in the earth, whether it be honour, pleasure, or riches, might be given me."[28]

With the publication of the New Testament, Tyndale next translated the Pentateuch; but on his way to Hamburg to print it, his ship was wrecked. All his manuscripts were lost, all his labor destroyed. Fortunately, Tyndale was joined in Hamburg by Miles Coverdale, who assisted him in retranslating the work and who would in time make many significant contributions to the translation of the Bible. Together they worked, and in January of 1530 the Pentateuch was printed in English, again with its printing source disguised. The Pentateuch too was shipped to England, and there it, too, was sought for burning.[29]

It was shortly after the Pentateuch arrived in England that certain individuals tried to persuade the king to bring Tyndale back to England in peace if he would agree to certain conditions. Tyndale was wary of the volatile situation in England but declared he would return if one condition was met — that the king would approve an English Bible of *some* sort for the people, if not his own. As a part of these negotiations, Tyndale revealed much of what he had suffered for the cause, including "poverty, . . . exile out of my natural country and bitter absence from my friends, . . . my hunger, my thirst, my cold, the great danger wherewith I am everywhere encompassed, . . . and hard and sharp fightings which I endure."[30] He insisted that death would be more pleasant than life if it were really true that men could not endure truth and that knowledge of the scriptures would bring more harm than good.

When negotiations failed, other attempts were made to bring Tyndale to England, though not so peacefully. Appeals were made to the German emperor to surrender him, and instructions were given to kidnap him. Living like a fugitive, he managed to elude his pursuers.[31]

Despite his frequent uprootings Tyndale continued to work and even to rework what he had already done. Nothing testifies so strongly of his desire to produce a faithful English version of the scriptures as do his efforts to improve his own previous translations. In 1534 there was printed "The Newe Testament dylyggently corrected and compared with the Greke by Willyam Tindale," and in 1535 "The Newe Testament yet once again corrected by Willyam Tindale" as well as revised editions of the Pentateuch. The corrections he made on the New Testament alone numbered in the thousands. Scholars generally agree that the changes were indeed for the better, lifting the good work he had done into the realms of excellence.[32]

But Tyndale's pen was soon immobilized. In 1535 he lived in Antwerp in a house established by English merchants. There he developed a close friendship with another Englishman, not realizing the friendship to be treacherous. So trusting had Tyndale become that he lent his friend forty shillings — just hours before he was betrayed by him into the hands of the emperor's soldiers. Tyndale was taken to Vilvorde Castle, just north of Brussels, where he was imprisoned.

He would never be freed from the dungeon there, suffering its isolated darkness and dampness for over sixteen months. While in prison, he wrote a touching letter which provides clues to his condition and state of mind:

> If I am to remain here during the winter, you will request the Procureur to be kind enough to send me from my goods which he has in his possession, a warmer cap, for I suffer extremely from cold in the head, being afflicted with a perpetual catarrh, which is considerably increased in this cell. A warmer coat also, for that which I have is very thin: also a piece of cloth to patch my leggings: my overcoat is worn out. He has a woollen shirt of mine, if he will be kind enough to send it. I have also with him leggings of thicker cloth for putting on above; he also has warmer caps for wearing at night. I wish also his permission to have a lamp in the evening, for it is wearisome to sit alone in the dark. *But above all, I entreat and beseech your clemency to be urgent with the Procureur that he may kindly permit me to have my Hebrew Bible, my Hebrew Grammar, and Hebrew Dictionary, that I may spend my time with that study.*[33]

Just two events brought Tyndale out of his dark dungeon. One was a bitter trial; another was an attempt to disgrace him by publicly stripping him of his ecclesiastical authority. Throughout his imprisonment he endured intense pressures to recant. Finally, on October 6, 1536, twelve years after he left England, he was led from prison to the stake. There he was strangled, then his body burned. He had time to utter one last cry: "Lord, open the King of England's eyes."[34]

It is one of the ironies of history that Tyndale died not knowing the battle was nearly won.

The Work of Coverdale and Others

In the 1530s, the political climate in England underwent many significant changes. Henry VIII had split with Rome to facilitate his divorce and remarriage, and Anne Boleyn, his new love, favored a translated Bible. Others also had come to see the folly of denying the scriptures to the people—including Sir Thomas More.[35]

Working behind the scenes to effect this change in policy were a number of enlightened men. One of these was Tyndale's assistant, Miles Coverdale. A man of peace, Coverdale established good friendships with men of all persuasions; Tyndale, More, and Cromwell all considered him a friend. In 1530, Coverdale had written Cromwell, patiently reasoning the need for an English scripture. Evidently, he helped influence Cromwell, because he later lent support to Coverdale to accomplish that work.[36]

Finally, in 1534, a group of prominent church authorities petitioned the king to allow scriptures in the English language. The king, always in touch with political expediency, responded positively, and a process was begun by which an "official" translation might be obtained. Some of those chosen to work toward that end, however, were actually obstructionists, and the project quietly died.

But while the "official" translation work was grinding to a halt, Coverdale secretly worked on his own version—a project supported by Cromwell. In making his translation, Coverdale used Tyndale's Pentateuch and New Testament, but improved upon them where he could, using his own natural sense for linguistic harmony and rhythm. The rest of the Old Testament Coverdale translated himself, referring for guidance to several other works, including Luther's Bible.[37]

Coverdale's accomplishment, the first *printed complete* English Bible, was published overseas and shipped to England. There were hopes this time for a favorable reception, based on changing opinion and a very flattering dedication to King

Henry, whom Coverdale compared to Moses and King Josiah in leading the people from darkness to light.

It is believed that Cromwell drew the king's attention to the new translation. The king, likely weary of ecclesiastical divisions and flattered by the dedication, asked the bishops for their opinions. They offered various criticisms, but Henry demanded, "Are there any heresies maintained thereby?" When they could point out none he exclaimed, "If there be no heresies, then in God's name let it go abroad among our people."[38]

The English people were at last free to purchase, own, and read a Bible without fear of retribution. Many received the new Bible warmly. But reluctance, even hostility, still lingered among a significant number of the clergy. Though they no longer had the power to seize or burn the scriptures, their strong disfavor worked against its universal acceptance.

When Coverdale's Bible came out, Tyndale was yet alive, in prison. Coverdale was aware of Tyndale's plight, and though not daring to use his name openly, made vague reference to his situation in the prologue to his Bible. He also revealed the forces that had brought him to finish Tyndale's work: "It was neither my labor nor desire to have this work put in my hand: nevertheless it grieved me that other nations should be more plenteously provided for with the Scripture in their mother tongue than we: . . . when I considered how great pity it was that we should want it so long, and called to my remembrance the adversity of them [Tyndale chiefly] which were not only of ripe knowledge but would also with all their hearts have performed that they began, if they had not impediment."[39]

So Coverdale finished what Tyndale began. Unlike others, who suffered death for their roles, Coverdale's diplomacy kept him alive, though he was forced into exile at least three times. Nevertheless, he was able to maintain deep respect from diverse parties, and thus wield a strong influence on several succeeding biblical translations. He revised and republished his own version in 1537, but it remained too much Tyndale's work to be widely accepted by the clergy.

In 1537 another version of the Bible mysteriously appeared. It is believed that after Tyndale's death, among his effects were found his translations of Joshua to 2 Chronicles. These were left to some of his friends. One of these men, John Rogers, put together a new Bible that consisted of all of Tyndale's translations, including these last ones, with Coverdale's translation from Ezra to Malachi. The book was meant to honor Tyndale, now deceased; but it was thought wisest not to prejudice the work with his name, which was still bitterly despised by many. Hence it was published as the translation of "Thomas Matthew," a false name.[40]

Strangely, whether or not it was known how much of this work was Tyndale's, the authorities granted it license as an approved version (though Tyndale's first publications were still under condemnation). There were several reasons for the license. The public obviously wanted an English Bible, and the petition of 1534 by church leaders requesting an authorized Bible had not yet been fulfilled. Indeed, because of opposition from certain bishops, Archbishop Cranmer, a moderate with leanings toward an English Bible, decided that to give license to this version would save face for both the crown and clergy, as they could go along with the pretense that it was "new." So Cranmer wrote a letter to Cromwell, saying of this work, which was almost wholly as Tyndale had written it, "you shall receyve by the bringer herof, a Bible in Englische, both of a new translacion and off a new prynte, dedicated vnto the Kinges Maieste. . . . So farre as I have redde thereof I like it better than any other translacion hertofore made."[41]

So now two versions of the Bible were available, though the people's ignorance and poverty still severely limited their distribution. The books were not used, read, or taught in churches, where the uneducated might learn and the poor might hear. But finally, even that barrier began to crumble.

As early as 1536, Cromwell had considered a decree that English Bibles be placed in every church; but the time was not ripe. For many, the Bible translations available were still not satisfactory. Conservative clergy particularly objected to pro-Protestant leanings in the notes of the Coverdale and Matthew Bibles. And so Cromwell began to envision a Bible worthy to be placed in churches—free from criticism, done with the very best of scholarship, and with an external beauty worthy of its place.[42]

Coverdale was picked for the task. But this time he was given every advantage. France was selected as the place for the work. There they could obtain the best quality of paper and printing. Cromwell saw that Coverdale had all the help he needed in the way of grammars, dictionaries, other scholarly resources, and a personal assistant.

Coverdale's work was indeed thorough. He used the Matthew Bible as his original source, making corrections wherever he felt best. If he found a translation better than one in his own previous work, he did not hesitate to set aside his own.

After much labor, the translation and printing neared completion. Then, just as it appeared that at last the way to an unhampered printing of the Bible had been won, the French authorities confiscated the work and ordered the printing stopped. Political relations between France and England had deteriorated, and the French inquisitor-general halted the work. Through diplomatic channels England finally obtained permission to bring the presses back to England, but without the printed sheets. Coverdale had managed to ship some home prior to the seizure, and some that had been sold as waste paper to a haberdasher were retrieved; but for the most part, the work had to be reprinted.

In 1539, the "Great" Bible was released. It was called "Great" because of its size—but it was splendid in other ways, too. Perhaps its only outward flaw was small hands appearing on the pages pointing at nothing. They were originally intended to signify explanatory notes. But the King, tired of controversy over notes, had forbidden their inclusion.

In 1538, prior to this Bible's actual publication, Cromwell had issued an injunction that every church keep a Bible for the people and that the people be freely allowed to read it. Though there is evidence that the Matthew Bible was sometimes used, the decree was in anticipation of the Great Bible; and when it was available, it became the Bible "appointed to the use of the churches."[43]

There are many interesting reports of reactions to this sudden exposure to the Bible. It was now available to people of all classes, and the great controversy had surely aroused immense curiosity about its contents. On the one hand, "it was wonderful to see with what joy this book of God was received not only among the learneder sort and those that were noted for lovers of the reformation, but generally all England over among all the vulgar and common people; and with what greediness God's word was read and what resort to places where the reading of it was. Every body that could bought the book or busily read it or got others to read it to them if they could not themselves, and divers more elderly people learned to read on purpose."[44]

The way had been opened, and the people responded. Those with enough money purchased the Great Bible for private use, then often read to crowds who gathered. But its cost of ten to twelve shillings prevented its availability to the majority, except at the churches. There the poorer flocked to marvel that they could see and hear and handle a *whole* Bible, printed in the English tongue.[45]

Nevertheless, there were still dark days ahead. In Henry's later years he turned against the Protestants. Cromwell was executed. Persecutions resumed. "The crafty, false, and untrue translation of Tyndale" (specifically the Matthews and Coverdale versions) were denounced and again publicly burned.[46] The Great Bible, also mostly Tyndale's work, was not attacked, but its reading by common people was again forbidden. These events were only the first of very turbulent times during which the opinion toward vernacular translations rose and fell precipitously.

During Edward's reign, Protestants returned to favor, and Bibles again were set up in the churches. Even weekly scripture reading in the churches was encouraged.

Then Mary Tudor came to power. Bitterly anti-Protestant, Mary sentenced readers of the English Bibles to death. Many of those instrumental in bringing about English translations lost their lives, among them Archbishop Cranmer and John Rogers.[47]

Coverdale and numbers of other Protestant leaders fled to the Continent, finding safety in Geneva, whence sprang yet another version of the Bible. But this was not just another version. A free intellectual climate had brought to Geneva some of the finest religious scholars in all of Europe. Drawing upon each other's knowledge and upon original sources not previously available, these scholars helped produce new translations of English, French, and Italian Bibles. In the English, they found the greatest need for revisions in that part of the Old Testament not done by Tyndale. By the time the Geneva Bible was ready for publication in 1560, Queen Elizabeth had replaced Mary on the throne, and she again allowed free access to English Bibles.

Because of its smaller size, its simplicity, and certain innovations that made it easier to read (namely Roman type rather than Gothic, and the use of verses), the Geneva became the most popular Bible for private use among the people. Indeed, it became the common family Bible for the next 50 years and was the Bible the Pilgrims carried to America. However, because of its Protestant bias in the marginal notes, it was never approved by the Church of England, although its high quality of scholarship was grudgingly conceded. The Great Bible remained the Bible of the churches.[48]

This awkward situation—one version of the scriptures in the homes but another in the churches—aroused the desire for yet another version. Thus, the plan that had once been suggested, that there be an "official" version done by ecclesiastical authorities of the church, was finally set into motion. Approximately sixteen men, mostly bishops, labored on this new translation. Here at last was hope for a version that would be accurate and non-controversial.

But while the "Bishops' Bible," as it was designated, did officially replace the Great Bible in the churches, it could not uproot the Geneva Bible in the hearts of the people. Although it did make improvements in a few areas, in general it was too uneven and too literal. The beauty of Tyndale's "Cast thy bread upon the waters," for example, had become "Lay thy bread upon wet faces."

The work that Tyndale began had through the years been taken up by many men. Each had sought to improve it, and indeed they had; a work so vast and challenging could hardly have been made perfect by one mere man. And yet, the amazing truth is that while Tyndale's work was eventually refined, it was of high quality from the start. Eighty to ninety percent of the biblical work Tyndale performed remains today in the form in which he set it.[49] In him was the gift of capturing accuracy in a rhythmically poetic way, thus adding beauty and power to the scriptural message.

While many circumstances combined to make the scriptures accessible to the English people, surely Tyndale's work, life, and death were among the chief factors. He gave for this cause all that he could give, for he knew in a very personal way the immeasurable worth of the scriptures; and he recognized that for these eternal jewels, no price was too great.

The translation Tyndale made of the Sermon on the Mount may well serve as the only epitaph he needs: "Blessed are they which huger and thurst for rightewesnes: for they shal be fylled. . . . Blessed are they which suffre persecucion for rightewesnes sake: for thers is the kingdom of heven. Blessed are ye whe men shall revyle you/and persecute you/and shal falsely saye all manner of evle sayings agaynst you for my sake. Reioyce ad be gladde/for greate is youre rewards in heven. For so persecuted they the prophetts which were before youre dayes."[50]

CHAPTER SEVEN

The Sweet and Ripened Fruit

The bloodshed in the late 1500s had a decidedly sobering effect on England. The outrageous spectacle of Protestants being martyred under one regime, and Catholics under another, helped prepare the way eventually for greater religious tolerance. Under James, who became king in 1603, a major move in that direction took place.

James faced a nation badly in need of religious unification. The Puritans had grown strong in numbers and also in determination to make their numbers felt, and they petitioned James for reforms. Though he was not sympathetic to the Puritan cause, James felt it politically wise to hold a conference to consider their grievances and did so the following year. It is surprising that the most remarkable accomplishment to come out of that three-day conference arose not from the carefully prepared petitions, which were generally rejected, but from one individual's seemingly extemporaneous suggestion—that there be a new Bible. The suggestion was made by John Reynolds, a leading Puritan and president of Corpus Christi College, who felt the Bible used in the churches was "corrupt and not aunswerable to the truth of the Originall."[1] Reynolds was not seeking a pro-Protestant version, however; he was seeking a *correct* Bible that would be satisfactory to all.

The majority of those in attendance were opposed to another translation. One participant remarked that there would never be an end to translations if everyone's whims were humored. But the person who really counted, King James, was very taken with the idea. It is true that part of his excitement over a new translation was due to his strong disapproval of the Geneva Bible. He was displeased not because of inaccuracies, but because of what he considered improprieties in its notes. But he also was excited at the idea of heading such a project—for King James liked books, and the Bible most of all.[2]

His boyhood tutor had acquainted him with the Bible, and he had discovered for himself its worth. In fact, he considered himself somewhat of a biblical scholar. He had translated a paraphrase of the book of Revelation and some of the Psalms, and in all his communications he made frequent references to the scriptures.

One writer points out that we should feel quite thankful that Reynolds's lonely request fell upon James's ear. Otherwise, such an idea probably would have died.[3] Indeed, when we consider the differing roads that various kings and queens have pursued to embellish and glorify their names, we can easily conclude that King James was among those who chose most wisely. Not only did James nurture this dream of a new Bible acceptable to all, but he also cared enough about the final product to carefully ensure its excellence.

The excitement King James felt about this project is shown in the rapidity with which he acted. Within one month, he had a detailed plan drawn up outlining how the work would be accomplished.[4] The translators were then chosen with care. Initially there were fifty-four of them, selected with a representative balance in mind—Anglicans and Puritans, high churchmen and low churchmen, clergy and laity, theologians and linguists.[5] James sincerely wanted a book for all people, regardless of religious preference, one to which no one would take offense.

Furthermore, he wanted it to be of highest scholastic quality. Among the men selected was the dean of Westminster, a master of fifteen languages with an unquestioned reputation for accuracy in scholarship. Another had spent thirty years as King's

Professor of Hebrew at Trinity College, Cambridge. Others were skilled in various combinations of Hebrew, Greek, Latin, French, Italian, and Spanish.[6]

But the committee possessed more than just linguistic acumen. Among its members were men of high character who exercised good influence on their peers in many ways. One was persistent in persuading fellow clergymen of the need to take the gospel abroad. Four were Puritan clergymen, some of whom had made enormous financial sacrifices for their faith. Another had gained wide-reaching respect for his meekness and charity, even toward his enemies. Still another had labored among the Scots, preparing ground necessary for unifying the Church of England and the Church of Scotland.[7] Reynolds himself, who had suggested the work, in the end sacrificed his life for it. Though he became ill, he insisted on giving his utmost to the project, thereby contributing to his own death.[8]

Though King James intended to give every support necessary to the translation, he was not wise in money matters and soon encountered an empty treasury. Undaunted, however, he appointed the Archbishop of Canterbury, Richard Bancroft, as a general manager of the project and suggested he raise funds for it from the bishops and clergy. But the appeal evidently fell on deaf ears. Finally, the universities agreed to provide, without charge, food and lodging for the translators while they worked. Some scholars also claim that a publisher promised to pay a sum for the right to print and sell the book. But it is generally felt that most of the translators did their work at considerable sacrifice to themselves and with little financial remuneration.[9]

One account given by a committee member, John Bois, to an associate captures the extent of that sacrifice. Bois indicated that he as a translator was secluded in his work throughout the week until Saturday evening, that he then went home on Sunday to take care of his most urgent clerical duties, and that he returned on Monday morning to resume translation. This kind of schedule he followed for four years.[10]

Although the committees had been appointed in 1604, formal work did not begin until 1607 because of the fund-raising delays. While fifty-four men supposedly were appointed, only forty-seven actually worked on the Bible, and several of them died before its completion. These forty-seven were divided into six groups. Two of the groups worked at Oxford, two at Cambridge, and two at Westminster. Each group was assigned a different section of the scriptures to translate.

The instructions they received through Bancroft were very strict. This work was to be a revision only, not a fresh translation, and the work they were to revise was the Bishops' Bible. They were granted permission, however, to refer to Tyndale's, Coverdale's, and the Geneva versions; and where any of those agreed more closely with the Hebrew and Greek texts that were available, they could use them instead.[11]

Evidently the scholars worked much more independently than these instructions indicate. For example, according to their own accounts, they consulted every translation or scholarly work currently available, including versions of the Bible in Spanish, French, Italian; the Vulgate and other Latin versions; Luther's and other German versions; as well as the best Aramaic, Hebrew, and Greek manuscripts then existing.[12] They even consulted the Rheims-Douai Version, which had recently been translated by Roman Catholic scholars in a defensive move against the Protestant translations. Because the Douai Version was still so heavily laden with Latin terminology, it did not have much effect on the King James, but the King James Version came to have much effect on later Douai versions.[13]

Thus, every source that might possibly give an insight into the *best* translation was eagerly sought. In fact, the translators sent appeals to all bishops to notify those who were skilled in ancient tongues, and who had information or observations that might be helpful to the translators, to forward that information to the appropriate college. And when there was difficulty over any obscure passage, the translators did not hesitate to make contact with outside specialists who might be able to shed some light upon its meaning.[14]

The process by which the translators obtained not just a coherent but an excellent translation, in spite of its being a many-handed work, was apparently quite unusual for the times. Each man began by working separately on his assigned chapters. Then the committee met for review. There is some uncertainty as to how this final correlation process was actually carried out, but John Seldon, who knew some of the translators, was quoted in 1689 as saying:

"The translators in king James's time took an excellent way. That part of the Bible was given him who was most excellent in such a tongue . . . and then they met together, and one read the translation, the rest holding in their hands some Bible, either of the learned tongues, or French, Spanish, Italian, etc. If they found any fault they spoke; if not, he read on."[15]

While some have questions about the full accuracy of this summary,[16] the fact that the King James Version is so beautifully lyrical—so pleasing to the ear—lends credence to this oral method of correlation.

In the March 1974 *Ensign*, Margaret Tuttle Sanchez illustrated the process with which one committee dealt with the problem of translating the Psalms. In her imaginative portrayal, one of the scholars begins by reading the scripture as existing in the Bishops' Bible:

> "God is my shepherd. . . . " "Wait!" There is a chorus of exclamation. . . . All present agree that "shepherd" is the correct meaning. But to begin by saying "God" is too abrupt. The rhythm is awkward. There is no melody to the line. Moreover, the Hebrew word is *Jehovah* that here and elsewhere Coverdale has translated as the LORD, using capital letters. And besides, the Book of Common Prayer and the Geneva Bible both agree that there is a superior wording: "The Lord is my shepherd."
>
> The reader continues: "Therefore I can lack nothing." This is better than the inversion in the Prayer Book, "Therefore can I lack nothing," but it does not equal the simplicity and power of the Geneva version, "I shall not want." This is it, a line with dignity and beauty of movement: "The LORD is my shepherd; I shall not want."
>
> Again, the Bishops' version is read: "He will cause me to repose my self in pasture full of grass." The Prayer Book (Great Bible) version states, instead, "He shall feed me in a green pasture." But why that future tense? Coverdale originally used the present tense, "He feedeth me." The Geneva text agrees on this point and contributes a valuable alternative: "He maketh me to rest in green pasture." "He maketh me"—how effectively the rhythm is enhanced by the alliteration. "To

what?" "Repose myself" and "rest" both suggest the same thing. But how else could it be said if the Lord were a shepherd and I were a sheep?

"He maketh me to *lie down*"—here the committee has had inspiration. The words are not in any of the English texts before them, but they agree to adopt them. "He maketh me to lie down in green pasture." "Why not green pastures?" a new voice asks. Perhaps one of the group has glanced at an English paraphrase . . . [by] Gilby published in 1580. . . .

"Green pastures" suddenly sounds universal. Coupled with the use of the present tense, the line takes on immediacy and significance for each follower of the Good Shepherd. It is accepted.

"And he will lead me unto calm waters." The future tense has already been vetoed. Geneva, Coverdale, and Gilby all say, "And leadeth me." Someone makes an astute observation: there is more balance and dignity if the "he" of the Bishops' Version is retained but all the "ands" are dropped. "He leadeth me"—it is a good beginning. There is a choice of prepositions: "to"? "unto"? "by"? "forth"? "beside"? "Beside" is chosen. Shall it be "calm waters," "the pleasant rivers of waters," "a fresh waters," "the waters of comfort"? The Geneva Version triumphs again with the quiet beauty and appropriateness of "the still waters." "Green pastures" and "still waters" now balance perfectly.

"He maketh me to lie down in green pastures: he leadeth me beside the still waters."

The line surpasses those of all earlier texts; it bears the stamp of excellence so characteristic of the King James Version.[17]

Because records are available of the other translations the committee used, we can tell from which of these the King James Version ultimately drew. What is important here is that although the translators were seeking accuracy, they were seeking far more than just that. To have sought accuracy alone would have been much easier, but they were also seeking what would be *spiritually satisfying*. They recognized that the true purpose of scriptures is to move—to motivate. Ideas placed in their best frame are far more stimulating and memorable. Because the committee members were often willing to expend the energies necessary to find the *best* word, the *most pleasing phrase*, they were able to conserve "all that was gracious and dignified and beautiful from the cherished versions of the past,"[18] and to blend them with inspiration into a glorious new whole. The result of that toil, that love, is a Bible that has had immense impact on every generation since its publication.

Actually, accuracy and beauty of phrasing were not left to just one committee. As one of the translators explained, "Neither did we disdain to revise that which we had done, and to bring back to the anvil that which we had [already] hammered."[19] Although there is some question as to whether it was fully carried out, the original plan was that each group's work be reviewed by every other group. If this plan was followed, the manuscript went through at least six or more revisions before it was actually published. We know for certain that there was at least one review—this by a committee of twelve, two from each of the six major groups, who met after the other committees had disbanded, at least for nine more months and perhaps longer, reviewing and revising the work as a whole.[20] The original plan had also called for final review and approval by the bishops, the Privy Council, and King James. In view of James's strong personal interest in the results, it would be surprising if at least some of these steps were not taken.

And so, in 1611, King James's Bible was completed. It is said he felt more pride in seeing this work accomplished than in a recent military victory over Spain. And he had every right to feel proud. The Bible was handsome—both inside and out. Of special satisfaction to him, no doubt, was its flattering dedication. But it was impressive for many other reasons as well, particularly for its beautiful new illustrations. In addition, it boasted a table of contents, various other tables of information, an almanac, a genealogical chart, and a map of Canaan. Each chapter had an introductory summation of contents and briefer summations at the top of each column. The chapters and verses were numbered.[21] While these kinds of features are common in our Bibles of today, in earlier times they were remarkably new.

One thing the Bible did not contain was controversial notes. James had been emphatic about this. The only notes allowed were those that explained Hebrew and Greek words or that gave alternative translations or referred the reader from one scriptural passage to another. "The text ought to speak for itself" was the policy adhered to.[22]

One feature that the original version possessed but that has been left out of subsequent editions was a lengthy preface titled "The Translators to the Readers." Believed to have been written by Dr. Miles Smith but approved by all, it reveals much insight into the hearts of the men who translated the Bible for us. Still mindful of the great struggles that had been waged in behalf of the Bible prior to this time, and of the still lingering negative opinions toward this new translation, the spokesman for the translators referred sadly to their "zeal to promote the common good," which "deserveth certainly much respect and esteem, but yet findeth cold entertainment in the world."[23]

The translators insisted that their only object was to make out of several good translations one final one that was better. They reaffirmed once more the great need for translation itself, stating that such work "openeth the window, to let in the light; . . . breaketh the shell, that we may eat the kernel; . . . removeth the cover of the well, that we may come by the water; even as *Jacob* rolled away the stone from the mouth of the well."[24]

Not only had the stone been rolled away, but every effort had been made to ensure that the water that came forth was in its purest, most refreshing form. In the King James Version, that water was a river, its fountainhead truth, fed by many streams and tributaries.

From the pens of the Hebrew prophets and Greek translators who had given physical shape to that truth, there had come homely but highly effective imagery—truth wrapped in images of wells and wildernesses; of shepherds and sheep; of sowing, cultivating, and harvesting; of oil and lamps, arks and threshing floors. The Hebrews had influenced the rhythmic poetry of the books, providing parallelism for its structures, giving it balance and contrast.

From the New Testament writers, who were influenced by Greek, had come a more flexible sentence structure and Greek customs and names. Even the English form of the name *Jesus Christ* was inherited from the Greek. From the Latin influence had come melody and deeply imbedded Latin terminology such as *justification, sanctification, dispensation*. From the Anglo-Saxon had come brevity in the form of one-syllable words. Over eighty percent of the Sermon on the Mount consists of one-syllable words, attesting to their Saxon origin.[25]

Of this inheritance from strong multiple sources one writer has observed, "It must suffice here to point out that the perennial glory of the King James Bible is that it succeeded so wonderfully in combining these diversified elements—some from Hebrew, some from Greek, some from Latin, some from Anglo-Saxon—and in fusing them into a unified and harmonious kind of speech."[26]

As the Bible's original shape came from several different cultures, so its final *English* form was the handiwork of many men. One writer explains that "the development of the English text was . . . a gradual unfolding. Each translation entered into the making of the one that came after it and was incorporated with it, thus transmitting its own influence down the whole line of descent."[27]

The English translation had begun with Wycliffe, and his influence remains upon it. The Geneva Bible translators had used the Wycliffe translation and so had passed on some of his work. Also, his precedent of simple structure and plainness of speech was a route that was consistently followed.

Tyndale, however, exercised the greatest influence. The entire line of Bibles that followed him were basically revisions of his first work. While it had been refined again and again by other hands, the work remained basically Tyndale's.

Coverdale had been the laborer behind the Great Bible and other versions. To him is attributed the Bible's final smoothness, an even-flowing tempo, and a special sweetness, contributions consistent with Coverdale's own basically gentle nature.

The Geneva Bible also had much influence. Because its writers had so diligently sought the Bible's pristine intent, searching newly discovered manuscripts previously unavailable to Tyndale, it added clarity in areas that had been obscure. It also added a vitality that had been part of the original; because of its fidelity to original tongues, its renderings often were highly poetic.[28]

The high-church origins of the Bishops' Bible are seen in

the elegance and high propriety found in some verses of the
scriptures. And it helped tone down some renderings of the
Geneva that were felt to be too sharp.[29]

Finally, there is the touch of those forty-seven translators
who produced the King James Bible. Charles Butterworth describes the impact of their sensitive and polished work: "Compared with its predecessors, the King James version shows a
superb faculty of selection and combination, a sure instinct for
betterment. . . . No doubt, the men of the six revising com-
panies were aided by the era wherein they worked; it was an
age in which there was a lively appreciation of literary skill. . . .

"[But] much was also required of the King James workmen
to know what they should preserve untouched in such a rich
inheritance."[30]

Perhaps the most precious gift bequeathed by *every* translator
who labored on the Bible—from Wycliffe to the forty-seven—
was their earnest care and love for it. This love and care is best
illustrated in the King James version by the following outline
of sources from one section of the Sermon on the Mount. (See
Matt. 6:28-33.) It should be realized, however, that in many
cases, a phrase attributed to one source may be distinctly different from Tyndale's version by only the change of one or two
words.

Tyndale: Consider the lilies of the field, how they grow;
King James: They toil not,
Coverdale: neither do they spin:
Great: And yet I say unto you,
Geneva: That even Solomon in all his glory
Coverdale: was not arrayed like one of these,
Great: Wherefore, if God so clothe the grass of the field,
Rheims Douai: Which today is,
Geneva: and tomorrow is cast into the oven,
King James: shall he not much more clothe you,
Tyndale: O ye of little faith? Therefore take no thought, saying,
Wycliffe: What shall we eat? or, What shall we drink?
Coverdale: or, Wherewithal shall we be clothed?
Bishops': (For after all these things do the Gentiles seek:)
Tyndale: for your heavenly Father knoweth that ye have need
  of all these things.

Geneva: But seek ye first the Kingdom of God,
Wycliffe: and his righteousness;
Bishops': and all these things shall be added unto you.[31]

Out of a full understanding of its history, and in deep appreciation of its artistry, readers have called the King James Version of the Bible a "miracle," a "masterpiece," a "literary wonder of the world."[32]

But while it was destined for greatness, when it first appeared, it received cold welcome—even vicious attacks. Some with axes to grind called it theologically incorrect, even blasphemous.[33] And many of the common people, their ears prejudiced to the Geneva, were uncomfortable with its unfamiliar sounds. In time, though, with greater acquaintance came greater appreciation. King James's Bible crept its way into the hearts of its readers and won the admiration of individuals of numerous religious faiths. It would become the chief religious influence in the lives of many men for centuries.

Nevertheless, there have been additional efforts to revise it. Two revisions of minor consequence were made in the 1600s. In 1769 a revision was made to modernize the spelling. It is this specific revision that is the King James Version of today.[34]

In even later times, as other old manuscripts have been discovered, as more is learned about ancient tongues, and as language usage has changed, there have come more versions of the Bible. Among the first of the major versions were the Revised Version (1881, 1885), the American Standard Version (1901), and the Revised Standard Version (1946).

However, the original manuscripts that have most heavily influenced these translations are manuscripts that lack material found in other ancient copies. The result, in some revisions, is insufficiently supported substitutions for or deletions of precious original truths. Among the most serious losses are phrases that verify Christ's divinity. President J. Reuben Clark, Jr., writing in 1956, documented the changes made in some of the earlier revisions and explained why many of the substitutions and deletions in these works are of such concern to Latter-day Saints.[35]

This is not to say that the translations President Clark mentions and the others available to us today are not helpful. Some of the newer versions since President Clark wrote are easier to read and incorporate translations of documents (some dating to the second century A.D.) unavailable to the King James revisers. However, the Church continues to hold to use of the King James Version because of its general soundness in doctrine, its relative accuracy in telling the life and mission of the Savior, its beautiful expression, and its wide popularity.[36]

In fact, the King James Version most likely can never be completely replaced *because* it is such a vital part of the heritage of English-speaking nations. Its language has become "part and parcel of our common tongue—bone of its bone and flesh of its flesh."[37] In one fifty-year period alone, this Bible was the source of more than eleven hundred titles of published books, a credit to its "terse and telling imagery."[38] And everywhere in our language are its unforgettable phrases: "the apple of his eye" (Deut. 32:10; see Ps. 17:8; Prov. 7:2), "the signs of the times" (Matt. 16:3), "a pearl of great price" (Matt. 13:46), "a labor of love" (1 Thes. 1:3), "straining at a gnat" (Matt. 23:24), "a thorn in the flesh" (2 Cor. 12:7).

The heritage of the King James Bible has been in far more than expressive language, however. One writer says of it: "It has been in life and death the guide of a billion hearts and minds. It has taught, consoled, enlightened, civilized and disciplined millions who have read little else. It has . . . astonished the learned, and formed the characters of those who have led."[39]

When the common man first began to desire the Bible during the long period it was denied him, one of the great arguments against his receiving it was that he would cheapen and debase it. Yet, the reverse has proven true. Man has not debased the Bible; the Bible has lifted man. It has enriched his language and lifted his hopes, his achievements, and his eternal perspective. Through all the centuries of its being written, compiled, and translated, this collection of sacred records has indeed proved to be a truly sweet and ripened fruit.

CHAPTER EIGHT

The Power of the Word

To produce Bibles in the most influential languages of the sixteenth century and to make them easily accessible to everyone was to unleash a powerful new force upon the earth. Indeed, we have not yet fully grasped the impact this accomplishment has already had upon the world. The first impact was unquestionably upon the Reformation, but its reforming influence has spanned all the intervening centuries and has had a far broader effect than we usually think.

First of all, the Bible has been a primary force behind man's search in Western civilization to purify his religion—to find the Lord's true gospel. When we read descriptions of the low levels to which religion once sank, where corruption and ignorance were predominant among leaders of the church, we recognize what great progress has been made since the time of the first printed vernacular Bibles. And that progress must be mainly attributed to scriptural influence—a "light" and a leavening influence upon the heart of every sincere Christian, as far as it is used.

The second great impact the Bible has had is its feeding of the spirit of freedom. Too often the credit is given to political influence. But the desire for civil freedom has been very much intertwined with and seeded by its religious counterpart.

Among the first successful settlers of America, for example, were Puritans who were inspired to search for the freedom to live and worship as they felt the Bible directed them. And many who followed them to America were driven by the same desire. We know through revelation that the Lord raised up certain individuals to help create a political framework in this new land where those desires for freedom might be fulfilled. (See D&C 101:80.) It is significant that first among the freedoms established by these men was freedom of religion: "Congress shall make no law respecting an establishment of religion, or prohibiting the free exercise thereof; or abridging the freedom of speech, or of the press; or the right of the people peaceably to assemble, and to petition the Government for a redress of grievance."[1]

Not only has the Bible influenced the establishment of freedom, it has exerted a mighty power on the hearts of leaders that they might respect and preserve those freedoms. George Washington believed that "it is impossible to rightly govern the world without God and the Bible."[2] Many other leaders in Western civilization have similarly turned to the scriptures for guidance in leadership, and many have recognized that not only they but the people themselves must draw their strength from the scriptures if freedom is to be preserved. Woodrow Wilson once said of the Bible, "I ask every man and woman in this audience that from this day on they will realize that part of the destiny of America lies in their daily perusal of this great book."[3]

As the influence of the scriptures continues to spread to all lands, so the hope continues that someday full liberty will be seen in all the earth for *all* its inhabitants.[4] The Bible inspires its readers to work steadily toward that goal, for ultimately, as it says, it is the truth that makes men free. (See John 8:32.)

A third major impact that the Bible has had is the role it has played in the restoration of the fulness of the gospel. We are familiar with the story. A young man named Joseph Smith, severely troubled by the religious confusions of his day, searched the Bible for solutions. He came upon this scripture in James's epistle: "If any of you lack wisdom, let him ask of God." (James 1:5.) As the Prophet said, "Never did any passage of scripture come with more power to the heart of man than this did at this time to mine. It seemed to enter with great force into every feeling of my heart. I reflected on it again and again. . . .

"At length I came to the conclusion that I must either remain in darkness and confusion, or else I must do as James directs, that is, ask of God." (JS-H 1:12-13.)

Outwardly, this was just an ordinary event in which a troubled boy turned to the scriptures for help. Spiritually, it was a moment anticipated and prepared for before the earth's creation. There was to be a restoration of the fulness of the gospel to prepare for the second coming of the Savior; and Joseph Smith, who had been foreordained for this purpose, would be the instrument of that restoration.[5] The Bible—now in his own language and at his fingertips—was a catalyst that led Joseph Smith to his prophetic role.

While the Bible served as a catalyst leading Joseph Smith to the Father and the Son and to the burden of his own mission, so it was a continual influence in helping him fulfill that mission. (JS-H 1:74.) Shortly after the organization of the Church, the Prophet was directed to begin a translation of the King James Version. This he did under the influence of the Spirit, clarifying many passages in the King James Bible. However, the significance of his work goes far beyond those vital and important clarifications. As Joseph Smith struggled and searched for the meaning of passages, he was troubled by many questions and was moved to seek the Lord for answers. The result was revelation after revelation of truths once contained in scriptural records but lost over the centuries of darkness. Such brief references in the Bible to lost sheep, baptism for the dead, and the three kingdoms of glory expanded to fully understandable concepts. Many of these revelations are now found in the Doctrine and Covenants and the Pearl of Great Price.

Joseph Smith was only the first in these last days to be led to the fulness of the gospel via the Bible. From the earliest days of the Church until the present, many seekers of biblical knowledge have experienced deep dissatisfaction with discrepancies between its teachings and entrenched Christian beliefs. Echoes of "other" truths in the testaments have made them restless—

and their restlessness has made them search—and further searching has led them to discovery. Thus, the Bible has been a powerful force in the gathering of Israel.

A fourth major impact of the Bible is the effect it has had on the moral character of its readers. John Richard Greene long ago wrote of the changes that it first brought to England: "No greater moral change ever passed over a nation than passed over England during the years which parted the middle of [Elizabeth's reign] and the meeting of the Long Parliament. England became the people of a book, and that book was the Bible. . . . Far greater than its effect on literature or social phrase was the effect of the Bible on the people at large. . . . The whole temper of the nation felt the change. A new conception of life and of man superseded the old. A new moral and religious impulse spread through every class."[6]

That force continues today. The power and influence of that message, which teaches God's creation of earth and man, of the preparations that preceded the coming of God's Son, of an Eternal love so great that this Son would take up man's burden of sin and lay down his life in exchange, of Christ's teachings of love and meekness, are slowly spreading into the darkest corners of the earth. And wherever those truths are accepted and practiced, the people experience a change for the better, and the groundwork is prepared for the reception of the fulness of the gospel.

Perhaps the strongest evidence of the power and influence of the biblical message lies in the witness of how bitterly it has been denounced—even in modern days. Adolph Hitler saw it as a threat to his ambitions and, among his own people, revised the New Testament and sought to destroy the Old.[7] In private he said, "Whether it is the Old Testament or the New, or simply the sayings of Jesus, it is all the same old Jewish swindle."[8] During his time of power, in some occupied lands, churches and their Bibles were burned.

Nevertheless, the Bible remained a fountainhead of strength for those Hitler could not break. One bishop from an occupied land who had been imprisoned for noncooperation said in retrospect of that period: "The Bible was the weapon of our souls. It was with us in suffering, it fought for us, and our foes feared it. Why did they hate that very old book? For the same reasons we ourselves loved it. . . . Because the Bible spoke to us as a voice closer to our trembling hearts than any other voice. . . . This small book is the charter of peace, the charter of freedom, the charter of the future life of mankind."[9]

The struggle still goes on. In parts of the world today, the Bible is still denied. In schools in certain lands the Bible is officially branded as "unscientific," a "collection of fantastic legends," and a "tool of imperialistic, capitalistic powers for subjugating backward, unknowing nations."[10]

But these very attacks are a testimony of its strength and power, and when people who have been denied it again gain access to its strength, the Bible is reembraced with a touching devotion. One man held as a prisoner behind the Iron Curtain said that when at last he was given a requested Bible, "I treated it as one treats a priceless possession, a thing of great value, a rare treasure. . . . It gave me strength and assurance for what to my knowledge at that time were the interminable years ahead."[11]

In spite of the continual war fought against the Word of God, the work of putting the Bible into *every* man's hands and into *every* language continues. The goal of the typical Bible society, usually a collaboration of numerous different Christian denominations, has been to take a translated Bible to every people—a work that deserves our praise and gratitude. The Church of Jesus Christ of Latter-day Saints at this time does not make translations of the Bible itself but chooses carefully a translation available in a particular language for use among its members who speak that language.

The translation of the Bible into non-European languages began very early. One of the first translations, a rendition in an American Indian dialect, was completed in 1663.[12] Since then the Bible, or portions of it, have been translated into so many languages that it has been called the "book of a thousand tongues," though its translations have now far exceeded a thousand. It has been translated into every major language, and the effort in more recent years has been to translate it into even the remotest dialects of the earth—in many cases into dialects where previously there was no *written* language at all.[13]

Obviously, this work is tedious and fraught with many obstacles. For example, it reportedly took almost a hundred years to produce an entire Bible in the Tibetan language.[14] Though such an interval is rare, "many years," is the common time required for each new translation.

But the sacrifices required are measured in far more than time alone. Translating the Bible into the language of a remote tribe usually requires that someone first take the trouble to live among those people in their primitive conditions—to win their trust, to learn their language, and to convince them that there is a gift of knowledge that will serve them well. Extreme care must attend each translation, for the idioms and customs of isolated peoples are often very different from those of the Hebrews who recorded the scriptures and from those who made the first translations. The translator must be carefully sensitive to the unique experience of each distinctive culture.

One example of the sensitivity required pertains to the Zanaki people, who live on the eastern shores of Lake Victoria in Tanzania. In translating the Bible there, it was found that only a thief would knock on the door of a Zanaki hut. If the thief then heard a movement within, he would run away. The good man does not knock, but rather calls to his friends inside. Respecting the implications of these customs, Revelation 3:20, which speaks of Christ knocking for entrance into our lives, was wisely rendered in the Zanaki language, "Behold, I stand at the door, and call."[15]

The experiences of Adoniram Judson, a Christian missionary who made the Burmese translation, is typical of the challenges modern-day Bible translators face. He explains: "When we take up a language spoken by a people on the other side of the earth, whose very thoughts run in channels diverse from ours, and whose modes of expression are consequently all new; when we find the letters and words all totally destitute of the least resemblance to any language we have ever met with, and these words not fairly divided, and distinguished, as in Western writing, by breaks, and points, and capitals, but run together in one continuous line, a sentence or paragraph seeming to the eye but one long word; when, instead of clear characters on paper, we find only obscure scratches on dried palm leaves strung together, and called a book; when we have no dictionary and no interpreter to explain a single word, and must get something of the language before we can avail ourselves of the assistance of a native teacher—that means work."[16]

The work of translation also cost Judson twenty-one months in prison because of the Burmese dislike for Europeans. While he was in prison he became concerned for the manuscript he had been working on. His wife hid it for a time in their house, but as the rainy season approached they feared it would be severely damaged by mold. Therefore they felt that the best place for it after all was with Judson in prison. Mrs. Judson hid it in a roll of hard cotton that was sewed into a pillow. Judson slept on this uncomfortable pillow for months—only to have it stolen from him. The thief later threw the contents of the pillow away, and by some great fortune these contents came into the hands of a Christian convert. Although he did not at first realize that what he had was the manuscript of the Bible translation, he kept it, only much later discovering the value of this treasure. The manuscript survived to obtain its hard-earned place in the Burmese Bible.[17]

Any story that deals with the sacrifices made in bringing the Bible to the nations of the world would be incomplete without mention of the many people from all faiths who have labored earnestly to bring better comprehension to its study. There are archaeologists, sifting through sands and ruins for clues that might enlighten us; there are those who have scoured high and low for ever more ancient manuscripts; there are those who refine their knowledge of important original languages; and finally there are those who struggle to decipher newly discovered manuscripts.

As in any field of study, there are occasional stumblings and misunderstandings, but the Bible itself continues to open up the understanding and vistas of man, and the cost of making that knowledge available to all should work in us an even greater gratitude for the scripture we have. Truly the Bible, in any language, "*is* profitable for doctrine, for reproof, for correction, for instruction in righteousness: that the man of God may be perfect, throughly furnished unto all good works." (2 Tim. 3:16-17.)

CHAPTER NINE

The Gift of Latter-day Light

As the Lord inspired his prophets in the various dispensations and revealed to them his word, so he has dispensed additional gifts of scriptural light in the latter days. The need for additional light or fleshed-out knowledge was revealed early while the Book of Mormon was in process of translation. From the things revealed to Nephi we learn that, while the Bible is very special, it is not whole: "The book that thou beholdest is a record of the Jews, which contains the covenants of the Lord . . . made unto the house of Israel; and it also containeth many of the prophecies. . . . When it proceeded forth from the mouth of a Jew it contained the fulness of the gospel of the Lord. . . . After the book hath gone forth . . . there are many plain and precious things taken away from the book." (1 Ne. 13:23-24, 28.)

The Lord had promised that in the latter days there would be a restitution of all things. (See Acts 3:21.) We know now that part of that restitution was to be knowledge once contained in, but lost from, the Bible. This knowledge has been restored through several different methods: (1) through the gold plates that were translated as the Book of Mormon; (2) through papyrus records that came into Joseph Smith's hands to become the Book of Abraham, now contained in the Pearl of Great Price;

(3) through Joseph Smith's inspired translation of the Bible; and
(4) through direct revelations to Joseph Smith, most of which
are now in the Doctrine and Covenants and Pearl of Great Price.
Each of these four bodies of revelation would restore portions
of knowledge lost from the Bible.

One of the contributions made by the Book of Mormon was
clarification (sometimes through fulfillment) of biblical prophecies. Because of that, Latter-day Saints need not puzzle over
many statements that cause confusion among other Christians.
Christ's statement, "Other sheep I have, which are not of this
fold: them also I must bring, and they shall hear my voice; and
there shall be one fold, and one shepherd" (John 10:16), refers
in part to the Nephites and Lamanites. Ezekiel's reference to a
stick written upon for Judah and a stick written upon for Joseph
has been fulfilled through the uniting of testimonies from the
Bible and the Book of Mormon, therefore truly becoming one
stick in God's hand. (Ezek. 37:15-19.) These two scriptures have
been made understandable largely through the Book of Mormon. Of this effect Dr. Hugh Nibley writes, "Just as the New
Testament clarified the long misunderstood message of the Old,
so the Book of Mormon is held to reiterate the messages of both
Testaments in a way that restores their full meaning."[1]

In addition to the Book of Mormon clarifying the Bible, the
Lord restored actual portions of lost scripture. According to the
History of the Church, the early Saints themselves began to
express considerable interest in biblical references to scriptures
that were not in their possession. Joseph Smith wrote, "The
common remark was, 'They are *lost books;*' but it seems the
Apostolic Church had some of these writings, as Jude mentions
or quotes the Prophecy of Enoch."[2]

In the establishment of the fullness of the gospel, some of
the writings of ancient prophets not contained in our Bible were
returned. These writings include the Book of Moses and the
Book of Abraham, now in the Pearl of Great Price, some
prophecies of Joseph of Egypt, presently in the Book of Mormon (see 2 Ne. 3), and some writings of John the Beloved and
John the Baptist, contained in the Doctrine and Covenants (see
D&C 7, 93:7-17).

Hugh Nibley has done extensive research to show us that

the writings of Moses and other patriarchs that were revealed to Joseph Smith parallel very closely manuscripts that bear the names of ancient patriarchs and that were unknown to the Western world during the time of Joseph Smith. Such ancient manuscripts were written in difficult foreign languages and buried in dusty Continental libraries, ignored by scholars of the world when Joseph produced his versions.[3]

Joseph Smith was also used as an instrument to purify the Bible through his work upon an inspired translation. As Robert J. Matthews has pointed out, since the publication of the King James Version in 1611, British and American scholars have attempted many revisions, among which are the Revised Standard Version, prepared by the National Council of Churches, and the New English Bible, published by Oxford University Press and Cambridge University Press. All of these attempts witness that there was a need for a purer Bible, a need recognized and stated also by Joseph Smith: "I believe the Bible as it read when it came from the pen of the original writers. Ignorant translators, careless transcribers, or designing and corrupt priests have committed many errors."[4]

While there are many other revisions of the King James Version, Joseph Smith's work of clarification was unique. His work was "not merely a clarification of languages, but rather it introduced several new concepts and historical events of biblical times that are not contained in the King James Version. . . . It appears that he supplied some of the missing parts which had been taken away from the Bible or which had been lost before it was compiled. Therefore, Joseph Smith's translation of the Bible was unique in inception, procedure, and content."[5]

In fact, it was actually during his work on the Bible that he received the Book of Moses and translated Matthew 24, adding several verses and clarifications from new parts of verses. Both bodies of scripture are contained in the Pearl of Great Price.

Overall, Joseph Smith returned lost material, rephrased material so as to remove contradictions, and made many clarifications in his translation, all of which was done under direction of the Spirit. Joseph's special ability to understand the scriptures seems to have been a gift from God, as indicated in his record of his and Oliver Cowdery's baptism: "We were filled with the

Holy Ghost, and rejoiced in the God of our salvation. Our minds being now enlightened, we began to have the scriptures laid open to our understandings, and the true meaning and intention of their more mysterious passages revealed unto us in a manner which we never could attain to previously, nor ever before had thought of." (JS-H 1:73-74.) Later, in a letter to William W. Phelps on July 31, 1832, Joseph Smith wrote, "We have finished the translation of the New Testament. Great and glorious things are revealed, we are making rapid strides in the old book [Old Testament], and in the strength of God we can do all things according to his will."[6]

In addition to the importance of the manuscript itself, the translation also brought about further knowledge pertaining to the fullness of the gospel. Dr. Matthews details some of the results of Joseph's work:

> Several significant doctrines revealed in this dispensation are inseparably connected with Joseph Smith's translation of the Bible. Few subjects are more prominent in the gospel than the age of accountability, the building of Zion, Adam's role in the gospel plan, the degrees of glory, and the doctrine of celestial marriage.
>
> It is likely that other important items also were revealed to the Prophet in connection with his work of translating the Bible. There is some evidence that much of what the Prophet knew about the ancient patriarchs, ancient councils and Church organizations, and other topics were revealed to him in the context of this work.
>
> The real *product* of the Prophet's work with the Bible, then, is not simply the manuscript that constitutes the JST, but also the many revelations and spiritual experiences that came to the Prophet (and from him to the Church) as a result of his work with the Bible. Both the manuscript of the JST and the additional revelations are important, but of these it would seem that the multitude of the specific revelations on doctrine are of the greatest significance. These give increased knowledge and clarity to items on priesthood, resurrection, premortal existence and such things, and also enrich our understanding of the ministries of Jesus, Adam, Enoch, Melchizedek, Abraham, Paul, Peter, and John the Baptist. One

can hardly have a clear perspective of the biblical record without these revelations.[7]

In spite of the many spiritual blessings that arose from Joseph's translation of the Bible, he constantly experienced barriers in his efforts to translate it and to get it published. Though the members of the Church at times supported the Prophet, there were a number of periods when such assistance was not forthcoming, and he then had to lay aside the work of translation to fulfill the needs of his family. For example, at a conference of the Church on October 25, 1831, the minutes show this statement: "Brother Joseph Smith Jr. said . . . that the promises of God was that the greatest blessings which God had to bestow should be given to those who contributed to the support of his family while translating the fulness of the Scriptures. . . . Further said that God had often sealed up the heavens because of covetousness in the Church."[8]

This problem was to continue throughout Joseph's life, as indicated in a letter dated March 1843 from Brigham Young to the Church: "[Joseph Smith] has but one thing to hinder his devoting his time to the spiritual interests of the Church, to the bringing forth of the revelations, translation, and history. And what is that? He has not provision for himself and family, and is obliged to spend his time in providing therefor." The Saints were asked to bring wheat, corn, beef, eggs, and "everything eatable at [their] command." Perhaps most interesting is the postscript: "P.S. Brethren, we are not unmindful of the favors our President has received from you in former days. But a man will not cease to be hungry this year because he ate last year."[9]

The Prophet was able to accomplish much in the actual work of translating, but his other duties and the lack of full support from the Saints prevented his publishing or completing the translation to his satisfaction before his death.

The work of Joseph Smith in providing us with the word of God has borne fruit a hundredfold in the lives of the Saints. The restoration and translation of lost scriptures, the addition of modern-day revelation, and the clarification of the Bible are all part of the Lord's promise to reveal the fullness of the gospel.

However, not until recent times has the vital step been taken of drawing together the divergent pieces of the scriptural puzzle.

For more than 150 years, Latter-day Saints have used many different editions of the King James Version of the Bible. Though the translation has been the same, study aids and explanatory notes have differed drastically from one edition to the next. Furthermore, none of the editions has fully utilized the knowledge available through latter-day revelation.

In the early 1970s proposals were made to have the curricula of adult classes and seminary and institute courses concentrate more heavily and systematically on the scriptures. Those who were preparing the various manuals felt a strong need for study aids in the Bible that would cross-reference scriptures to the other standard works. Much of this early work came from the grassroots level and was channeled through the newly organized Internal Communications Department, which was then managed by J. Thomas Fyans (later called to be a General Authority). The advisers to this department—Elders Thomas S. Monson, Boyd K. Packer, and Marvin J. Ashton of the Council of the Twelve—took the recommendations to the Twelve and the First Presidency, and in mid-1972 they received the approval and blessing of President Joseph Fielding Smith. The three advisers were subsequently appointed to serve as the Scriptures Publication Committee (Elder Ashton was later replaced by Elder Bruce R. McConkie).[10] That fall a letter was sent to two scholars at Brigham Young University, inviting them to serve on a committee to begin preparing "a King James Bible which would include a standardized concordance, dictionary, atlas, and index, and . . . footnotes, ready references, and cross references related to other L.D.S. scriptures."[11] The scope of the work was later expanded to include similar study aids for the books in the Triple Combination.

As the project got underway, scholars in ancient languages and latter-day scriptures, professionals in editing and publishing, and experts in computer technology added their efforts. Their labor covered seven years and resulted in two truly outstanding works of light: the 1979 Latter-day Saint edition of the King James Version of the Bible and the 1981 edition of the Triple Combination. [12]

The new edition of the Bible has many unique features, including the following: new summary headings for every chapter of every book in the Old and New Testaments; extensive footnotes cross-referenced to all the Standard Works; topical guide and concordance with more than 2300 subject headings; a Bible dictionary that includes modern-day revealed knowledge; footnotes with verses from the Joseph Smith Translation that differ significantly from the King James Version; and twenty-four pages of full-color maps with a gazetteer.

The Triple Combination includes a greatly expanded and combined index for the Book of Mormon, Doctrine and Covenants, and Pearl of Great Price; new introductions to each of the three Standard Works; new summary headings for every chapter and section in the three books; four Church history maps, two new sections, and the 1978 revelation on the priesthood in the Doctrine and Covenants; and changes in some verses in the Book of Mormon and Doctrine and Covenants to correct errors made in previous printings.

One of the great problems in Christendom is the tendency for sects to establish doctrine based on isolated scriptures. Keeping in perspective *all* that the Lord has said about any principle is actually more useful and enlightening. One method of keeping proper balance and perspective is to read scriptures as a unified whole, making constant reference to related material. The new LDS editions of the scriptures help in that area more than any other Bible edition possibly could. The new system of footnote references is designed to unify God's word as well as to elucidate the relationships between passages of scripture. It also helps by providing other possible translations of the original Greek and Hebrew, by noting the word meanings that have changed since the first publication of the King James Version, and by referring the reader to translative changes made by Joseph Smith.

An excellent example of how this system works is in the account of Christ's baptism, contained in Matthew 3:13-17. Within that five-verse span, there are fourteen references to entries in the Topical Guide at the back of the edition, including "Jesus Christ, Baptism of" and "Holy Ghost, Dove, Sign of." There are also five immediate scripture references to related passages in the Gospels, the Book of Mormon, and the Pearl of Great Price. A significant variation in the Joseph Smith Translation is noted, and, since the variation is quite lengthy, it is printed in the back of the edition in its entirety rather than at the bottom of the page.[13] "Suffer" and "becometh us" have alternate Greek readings of "Permit it now" and "is fitting for us." The word "straightway" is listed with the Greek meaning of "immediately." Not only do the references clarify the meaning, but they also provide the means to do an extended study on the topic.

The Topical Guide adds nearly 600 pages to the Bible. Each entry gives related subject headings, then a list of scripture references, with a part of each scripture quoted or paraphrased. The pertinent word is italicized. In the above reference to "Jesus Christ, Baptism of," seven additional references with phrases are given. The overall topic of Jesus Christ is divided into fifty-seven categories, with thousands of scriptural references.

The index in the Triple Combination is now one complete index of 416 pages. In previous editions of the Triple Combination, each standard work had its own index, with references limited to the book it was attached to. The indexes to the Book of Mormon, Doctrine and Convenants, and Pearl of Great Price were combined and expanded for the 1981 edition. For instance, the previous Book of Mormon index entry for "God" lists only ten scriptures, whereas the present edition breaks the entry into thirteen categories, such as "God, Foreknowledge of" and "God, Power of," that contain eight pages of scripture references. The index also contains a marking system for names of people and places. The word *Nephi* has nine entries: the individuals are identified through lineage and dating, with additional entries for city, land, people, and plates.

Such extensive cross-referencing as these new editions of the scriptures entail was extremely difficult to accomplish before the 1970s. The *Strong's Exhaustive Concordance to the Bible*, which lists every word and every citation from the Bible, was first published in 1890 and took 100 men thirty years to compile.[14] The computer was thus necessary to the work; and even with modern technology, the cross-referencing took numerous assistants over six years to complete.[15] Truly this is an instance of the Lord's promise: "I will hasten my work in its time." (D&C 88:73.)

The printing of the Standard Works was an arduous process too. The search for a suitable printer eventually led to Cambridge University Press. The press had been printing Bibles since 1611 and had the facilities to accommodate the unusual requirements of the new editions. For example, the company developed a special typeface that shortened the descending and ascending lines of such letters as *d* and *y*. This shortened the extra spacing between lines that is usually required, reducing the overall length of the Bible considerably. Even so, the LDS edition of the Bible totals over 2,400 pages.

The university press also uses a method of printing known as monotype, one of the few printers still doing so. This old-fashioned system of printing is necessary in its work of printing Bibles. Since each letter and punctuation mark is a separate piece of metal, monotype allows for the minute adjustment needed when narrow columns, several different sizes of type, and extensive footnotes all appear on each page.[16]

The LDS edition of the Bible, when printing was completed, was so impressive that Cambridge University Press won the top graphics award for typesetting excellence in England for 1980 for its work on the book.[17] Roger Coleman, publishing director of Bibles and religious books for the press, echoed the feeling of many when he said, "Nothing is perfect in this world, . . . but *this* Bible is as nearly perfect as human beings can manage."[18]

These new editions of the scriptures certainly are unique in many respects. But they also share a common thread running through all work on the scriptures since the time of Adam. The love for the word of God has induced countless men and women to give their best efforts, to make their work on holy writ "as nearly perfect" as possible. Each time the Lord has worked through man to make his word available to a people, it is as if a great light has been shed upon them—the revelation of Christ himself. Isaiah says it this way: "The people that walked in darkness have seen a great light: they that dwell in the land of the shadow of death, upon them hath the light shined."(Isa. 9:2.) No wonder Peter exclaimed, "Ye should shew forth the praises of him who hath called you out of darkness into his marvellous light." (1 Pet. 2:9.) Surely when we understand how we got the Bible, we will find it easier to follow the Lord's admonition in Deuteronomy 11:18: "Therefore shall ye lay up these my words in your heart and in your soul."

Conclusion

Throughout this book we have tried to trace those forces that have unitedly worked to channel God's teachings to his children. In our tracings we have particularly sought to emphasize the love and sacrifice behind those labors. But we have of necessity portrayed as well the counter movements seeking always to inhibit the spread and effectiveness of Jehovah's word.

Ironically, at a time when the best and most useful edition of the Bible is available, the Bible is still suppressed in much of the world. Where there is free access to it, its voice of influence struggles to be heard over constant bombardments of false ideologies.

While free access to the Bible has indeed caused it to suffer somewhat from abuse and misunderstanding, it has unquestionably suffered most from abandonment. Its messages, however, are abandoned at great peril, for it represents eternal truth—truth passed down from the very Creation, truth added upon and reinforced with experience, truth revealed through word and deed beforehand, truth shaped in unforgettable language, truth personified in Jesus Christ, truth now bound together and illuminated with latter-day light, truth in constant struggle against untruth. And ultimately, it will be truth unconquered and unconquerable. Every gift of love and sacrifice that has been offered to relay that truth to men shall not have been given in vain.

Notes to Chapter 1

1. Millicent J. Taylor, *Treasure of Free Men* (New York: Harper & Bros. Publishers, 1953), p. 4.

2. Hugh W. Nibley, "Genesis of the Written Word," in *Nibley on the Timely and the Timeless* (Provo, Utah: Brigham Young University, 1978), p. 104.

3. Ibid., pp. 104, 119, 122.

4. Ibid., p. 112.

5. Ibid., p. 122.

6. R. K. Harrison, *Introduction to the Old Testament* (Grand Rapids, Michigan: William B. Eerdmans Publishing Co., 1969), pp. 546-47.

7. See Nibley, "To Open the Last Dispensation: Moses Chapter 1," in *Nibley*, pp. 2-19.

8. See Hugh W. Nibley, *Since Cumorah* (Salt Lake City, Utah: Deseret Book, 1967), p. 58, and *The Making of the Old Testament*, ed. Enid B. Mellor (Cambridge: At the University Press, 1972), pp. 5-8.

9. See Harrison, p. 94.

10. See Bruce R. McConkie, *Mormon Doctrine* (Salt Lake City, Utah: Bookcraft, 1966), p. 354.

11. See Hugh W. Nibley, *Abraham in Egypt* (Salt Lake City, Utah: Deseret Book, 1981), p. 4.

12. Nibley, "Genesis of the Written Word," p. 112.

13. P. R. Ackroyd and C. F. Evans, eds., *The Cambridge History of the Bible*, 3 vols. (Cambridge: At the University Press, 1970), 1:126.

Notes to Chapter 2

1. Geddes MacGregor, *The Bible in the Making* (Philadelphia: J. B. Lippincott Co., 1959), p. 48.

2. *Ancient Egypt: Discovering Its Splendors* (Washington, D.C.: National Geographic Society, 1978), p. 141.

3. Ibid., p. 140.

4. Moshe Pearlman, *In the Footsteps of the Prophets* (New York: Thomas Y. Crowell Co., 1975), prologue, p. 7.

5. Sidney B. Sperry, *The Spirit of the Old Testament* (Salt Lake City, Utah: Deseret Book, 1980), p. 23.

6. G. L. Robinson and Dillman, as cited by Sperry, p. 170.

7. Sperry, p. 93.

8. Ibid., p. 82.

9. See Avraham Gileadi, *The Apocalyptic Book of Isaiah* (Provo, Utah: Hebraeus Press, 1982), pp. 171-89.

10. For examples of Hebrew poetic structures and double meanings, see Victor L. Ludlow, *Isaiah: Prophet, Seer, Poet* (Salt Lake City, Utah: Deseret Book, 1982), pp. 31-39, 53-54, 56.

11. Theodore H. Robinson, as cited by Sperry, p. 60.

12. Herbert L. Willett, as cited by Sperry, p. 204.

13. G. L. Robinson, as cited by Sperry, p. 141.

14. See A. A. MacIntosh, "From the Ancient Languages to the New English Bible," in *The Making of the Old Testament*, ed. Enid B. Mellor (Cambridge: At the University Press, 1972), p. 154.

15. Ibid., pp. 154-55.

16. *Josephus: Complete Works*, tr. William Whiston (Grand Rapids, Michigan: Kregel Publications, 1960), p. 249.

17. Ibid., p. 250.

18. Harry Thomas Frank, Charles William Swain, and Courtlandt Canby, *The Bible through the Ages* (New York: The World Publishing Co., 1967), p. 72.

19. See MacIntosh, p. 148.

20. See Hugh W. Nibley, "A Strange Thing in the Land: The Return of the Book of Enoch," *Ensign*, July 1976, p. 65.

21. See MacIntosh, pp. 148-49.

22. R. K. Harrison, *Introduction to the Old Testament* (Grand Rapids, Michigan: William B. Eerdmans Publishing Co., 1969), p. 233.

23. See P. R. Ackroyd and C. F. Evans, eds., *The Cambridge History of the Bible*, 3 vols. (Cambridge: At the University Press, 1970), 1:132-33.

24. See Fred Gladstone Bratton, *A History of the Bible* (Boston: Beacon Press, 1959), pp. 122-24.

25. See Margaret Barker, "Other Writings of the Jewish Community," in *The Making of the Old Testament*, pp. 75-104.

26. See Bratton, p. 226, and Shemeryahu Talmon, "The Old Testament Text," in *The Cambridge History*, 1:162-63.

27. See MacIntosh, pp. 143-44.

28. See H. G. G. Herklots, *How Our Bible Came to Us* (New York: Oxford University Press, 1954), pp. 38-39.

29. See MacIntosh, pp. 144-45.

30. See Talmon, p. 162.

31. MacIntosh, p. 45.

32. Pearlman, prologue, pp. 7-8.

Notes to Chapter 3

1. See Irving Francis Wood and Elihu Grant, *The Bible as Literature* (New York: Abingdon Press, 1914), p. 232.

2. See Fred Gladstone Bratton, *A History of the Bible* (Boston: Beacon Press, 1959), pp. 165-66.

3. *The Bible Reader's Manual, a Supplement to the King James Version of the Holy Bible* (Glasgow, Scotland: Collins Clear-Type Press, 1959), p. 58.

4. Wood and Grant, p. 253.

5. See Harry Thomas Frank, Charles William Swain, and Courtlandt Canby, *The Bible through the Ages* (New York: The World Publishing Co., 1967), p. 127.

6. See Richard L. Anderson, "Types of Christian Revelation," in *Literature*

of Belief (Provo, Utah: Religious Studies Center, Brigham Young University, 1981), p. 61.

7."Clement of Rome's Letter to the Church at Corinth," tr. C. C. Richardson, in *A History of Christianity: Readings in the History of the Early and Medieval Church*, ed. Ray C. Petry (Englewood Cliffs, New Jersey: Prentice-Hall, 1962), p. 7.

8. See J. R. Dummelow, ed., *A Commentary on the Holy Bible* (New York: The MacMillan Company, 1936), p. 1057.

9. Bruce R. McConkie, *Doctrinal New Testament Commentary*, Vol. 3 (Salt Lake City, Utah: Bookcraft, 1973), pp. 371-72.

10. Maynard Mack, general ed., *World Masterpieces*, Vol. 1 (New York: W. W. Norton and Co., 1956), p. 2.

Notes to Chapter 4

1. Hugh W. Nibley, *Since Cumorah* (Salt Lake City, Utah: Deseret Book, 1967), pp. 33, 103.

2. Fred Gladstone Bratton, *A History of the Bible* (Boston: Beacon Press, 1969), pp. 190-95.

3. Frederick C. Grant, *Translating the Bible* (Greenwich, Conn.: The Seabury Press, 1961), pp. 16, 31.

4. Geddes MacGregor, *The Bible in the Making* (Philadelphia: J. B. Lippincott Co., 1959), pp. 69-70.

5. Ibid., pp. 61-63.

6. Ibid., pp. 87-88.

7. As quoted by H. G. G. Herklots, *How Our Bible Came to Us* (New York: Oxford University Press, 1954), p. 96.

8. Herklots, p. 96.

9. Harry Thomas Frank, Charles William Swain, and Courtlandt Canby, *The Bible through the Ages* (New York: The World Publishing Co., 1967), p.131; Herklots, p. 81.

10. MacGregor, pp. 90-92.

11. Herklots, p. 81; MacGregor, pp. 90-92.

12. Bratton, pp. 285-89; Enid B. Mellor, *The Making of the Old Testament* (Cambridge: At the University Press, 1972), pp. 185-89.

13. Ibid., p. 287.

14. Ibid., pp. 287-88.

15. Ibid., pp. 287-89.

16. Mellor, pp. 188-90; Bratton, pp. 290-93.

17. Bratton, p. 292.

18. Ibid., pp. 292-93.

19. Herklots, pp. 120-21.

20. Mellor, p. 190.

21. Margaret Deanesly, *The Lollard Bible and other Medieval Biblical Versions* (Cambridge: Cambridge University Press, 1920), p. 27.

22. Herklots, p. 82.
23. MacGregor, pp. 90-93.
24. Ibid., pp. 93-94.
25. Ibid., p. 95.
26. Bratton, p. 195.
27. Ibid., p. 195.
28. See D&C 91 for the word of the Lord to Joseph Smith concerning the Apocrypha.
29. Nibley, p. 103.
30. Grant, pp. 36-37.
31. David Daiches, *The King James Version of the English Bible* (Chicago: University of Chicago Press, 1941), p. 89.
32. Grant, p. 42.
33. Ibid., pp. 41-42.
34. H. W. Hoare, *The Evolution of the English Bible* (London: John Murray, 1902), p. 236.
35. Bratton, p. 296.
36. Herklots, p. 46.
37. Frank, Swain, and Canby, p. 148.
38. MacGregor, p. 103.

Notes to Chapter 5

1. Josiah H. Penniman, *A Book about the English Bible* (Philadelphia: University of Pennsylvania Press, 1931), p. 323.
2. Bede, *Ecclesiastical History*, 4 vols. (New York: AMS Press, Inc.), 4:172.
3. F. F. Bruce, *History of the Bible in English* (New York: Oxford University Press, 1978), p. 1.
4. Bede, 4:217-18.
5. H. G. G. Herklots, *How Our Bible Came to Us* (New York: Oxford University Press, 1954), p. 66.
6. Margaret Deanesly, *The Lollard Bible and other Medieval Biblical Versions* (Cambridge: University Press, 1920), p. 135.
7. Herklots, p. 63.
8. F. M. Stenton, *Anglo-Saxon England* (Oxford: At the Clarendon Press, 1967), p. 177; italics added.
9. Deanesly, p. 372.
10. Ibid., p. 26.
11. As quoted in Deanesly, pp. 26-27.
12. Deanesly, p. 27.
13. Ibid., p. 61.
14. Ibid., p. 62.
15. Edgar J. Goodspeed, *The Making of the English New Testament* (Chicago: University of Chicago Press, 1925), p. 1; Deanesly, pp. 36-48. For example, Deanesly cites this decree made in 1233 in Spain: "No man shall possess books of the Old or New Testament in Romance, and if any possess such let

them hand them over . . . to be burnt." If the books were not relinquished, the possessors of the books were themselves destroyed.

16. Deanesly, p. 39.

17. H. W. Hoare, *The Evolution of the English Bible* (London: John Murray, 1902), pp. 74-75.

18. Fred Gladstone Bratton, *A History of the Bible* (Boston: Beacon Hill Press, 1959), pp. 246-47.

19. Hoare, p. 77.

20. Ibid., p. 86; Bruce, p. 12.

21. Deanesly, pp. 225-28; Bruce, pp. 12-13.

22. Ira Maurice Price, *The Ancestry of Our English Bible* (New York: Harper and Row, 1956), p. 235.

23. Bruce, p. 12.

24. Frederick C. Grant, *Translating the Bible* (Greenwich, Conn.: The Seabury Press, 1961), p. 55; Penniman, pp. 337-39.

25. As quoted in Charles C. Butterworth, *The Literary Lineage of the King James Bible* (Philadelphia: University of Pennsylvania Press, 1941), p. 28.

26. Bruce, p. 1.

27. Hoare, p. 101; Baruch is an apocryphal book that was subsequently deleted with the rest of the Apocrypha from the King James Version.

28. Ibid., pp. 90-91.

29. Ibid., p. 61.

30. Bratton, p. 248.

31. As quoted in Bruce, p. 19.

32. As quoted in Bruce, p. 20.

33. As quoted in Goodspeed, p. 122.

34. John Foxe, *Book of Martyrs,* ed. W. Grinton Berry (Grand Rapids, Michigan: Baker Book House, reprinted 1980), p. 86.

35. Millicent J. Taylor, *Treasure of Free Men* (New York: Harper & Brothers, 1953), p. 8.

36. Deanesly, p. 334.

37. Price, p. 236.

38. Deanesly, p. 365.

39. Bruce, pp. 22-23.

40. Deanesly, p. 107.

41. As quoted in Deanesly, p. 24.

42. See Herklots, p. 56.

43. Deanesly, pp. 188-204; Herklots, pp. 43-46. There were some dedicated biblical scholars among the highest orders of the clergy, but in the lower classes, particularly among the parish priests, biblical knowledge was very scant. Beryl Smalley, in *The Study of the Bible in the Middle Ages* (Oxford: At the Clarendon Press, 1941), pp. 222-25, describes some of the reasons why study of the scriptures by the clergy themselves was not always considered important.

44. Deanesly, p. 93.

45. Ibid., pp. 118-19.

46. Ibid., pp. 372-73.

47. Wycliffe's translation says that "earth" was made "of nought." It should be remembered that his translation was made from the Latin Vulgate. Subsequent translations made from the Hebrew do not support his translation.

48. As quoted in Hoare, p. 104; this excerpt contains some modernized spelling.

Notes to Chapter 6

1. Douglas C. McMurtrie, *Wings for Words: The Story of Johann Gutenberg and His Invention of Printing* (New York: Rand McNally and Co., 1940), pp. 93-153.

2. F. F. Bruce, *The English Bible: A History of Translations from the Earliest English Versions to the New English Bible* (London: Oxford University Press, 1970), p. 26.

3. Frederic Seebohm, *The Oxford Reformers*, third edition (New York: Longmans, Green, and Co., 1913), pp. 312-16.

4. Ibid., pp. 317-18.

5. H. G. G. Herklots, *How Our Bible Came to Us* (New York: Oxford University Press, 1954), p. 25.

6. W. E. Campbell, *Erasmus, Tyndale and More* (London: Eyre and Spottiswoode, 1949), chapters 1-5 and 20. Also see Seebohm, pp. 454-58. Erasmus did come to be despised by many. Geddes MacGregor in *The Bible in the Making* (Philadelphia: J.B. Lippincott Co., 1959), p. 117, reports that one priest hung Erasmus's picture near his desk so he could spit upon it when he wished.

7. Edgar J. Goodspeed, *The Making of the English New Testament* (Chicago: University of Chicago Press, 1925), p. 3.

8. Ibid., pp. 3-4.

9. Foxe, *Book of Martyrs*, ed. W. Grinton Berry (Grand Rapids, Mich.: Baker Book House, 1980), p. 135.

10. Charles C. Butterworth, *The Literary Lineage of the King James Bible* (Philadelphia: University of Pennsylvania Press, 1941), p. 56.

11. Bruce, p. 29.

12. Butterworth, pp. 56-57.

13. C. H. Williams, *William Tyndale* (Stanford: Stanford University Press, 1969), p. 16.

14. Frederick C. Grant, *Translating the Bible* (Greenwich, Conn.: The Seabury Press, 1961), p. 62.

15. Enid B. Mellor, ed., *The Making of the Old Testament* (Cambridge: At the University Press, 1972), p. 192.

16. H. W. Hoare, *The Evolution of the English Bible* (London: John Murray, 1902), pp. 142-43; MacGregor, p. 117.

17. David Daiches, *The King James Version of the English Bible* (Chicago: University of Chicago Press, 1941), p. 8.

18. MacGregor, p. 118.

19. Bruce, p. 40.
20. Hoare, p. 145.
21. Ibid., p. 147.
22. Ibid., p. 144.
23. Bruce, p. 38.
24. Ibid., pp. 37-38.
25. Ibid., p. 39.
26. Williams, pp. 23-27; MacGregor, p. 118.
27. Bruce, pp. 39-40.
28. Ibid., p. 40; Hoare, p. 107.
29. Butterworth, p. 61; Fred Gladstone Bratton, *A History of the Bible* (Boston: Beacon Press, 1959), p. 251.
30. Williams, pp. 39-42.
31. Ibid., pp. 42-43.
32. Bruce, pp. 43-44.
33. Herklots, pp. 16-17.
34. Bruce, pp. 51-52.
35. Butterworth, pp. 71-73.
36. Ibid., pp. 94-95.
37. Ibid., pp. 95-97.
38. Bruce, p. 56.
39. Ibid., p. 58.
40. Bratton, p. 253; Daiches, pp. 26-27.
41. Butterworth, p. 111.
42. Ira Maurice Price, *The Ancestry of Our English Bible,* third revised edition by William A. Irwin and Allen P. Wikgren (New York: Harper and Row, 1956), pp. 256-58.
43. Bratton, pp. 254-55.
44. Goodspeed, p. 23.
45. MacGregor, p. 129.
46. Bruce, p. 78.
47. Bratton, p. 256; Butterworth, p. 149.
48. Bratton, pp. 257-58; MacGregor, pp. 132, 187.
49. Butterworth, p. 233.
50. Grant, p. 64.

Notes to Chapter 7

1. Charles C. Butterworth, *The Literary Lineage of the King James Bible* (Philadelphia: University of Pennsylvania Press, 1941), p. 206.
2. F. F. Bruce, *History of the Bible in English* (New York: Oxford University Press, 1978), p. 96.
3. H. W. Hoare, *The Evolution of the King James Bible* (London: John Murray, 1902), p. 244.

4. Frederick C. Grant, *Translating the Bible* (Greenwich, Conn.: The Seabury Press, 1961), p. 70.

5. Fred Gladstone Bratton, *A History of the Bible* (Boston: Beacon Press, 1959), pp. 261-62.

6. Geddes MacGregor, *The Bible in the Making* (Philadelphia: J. B. Lippincott Co., 1959), pp. 164-78.

7. Ibid., pp. 164-78.

8. Ibid., pp. 169-70.

9. Ibid., pp. 148-49; Bruce, p. 98.

10. Anthony Walker, *Life of John Bois: Translating for King James; Notes Made by a Translator of King James;* tr. and ed. Ward Allen (Nashville, Tenn.: Vanderbilt University Press, 1969), p. 139.

11. MacGregor, p. 163.

12. Butterworth, pp. 216-17; MacGregor, p. 163.

13. Edgar J. Goodspeed, *The Making of the New Testament* (Chicago: University of Chicago Press, 1925), p. 36; Butterworth, pp. 195, 203-4.

14. MacGregor, pp. 162-63.

15. Butterworth, p. 214.

16. Ibid.

17. Margaret Tuttle Sanchez, "How the Psalms Were Prepared for King James," *Ensign,* March 1974, p. 39.

18. Ibid., p. 40.

19. See J. Reuben Clark, Jr., *Why the King James Version* (Salt Lake City, Utah: Deseret Book, 1979), p. ii.

20. S. L. Greenslade, ed., "English Versions of the Bible," in *The West from the Reformation to the Present Day,* Vol. 3 of *Cambridge History of the Bible,* 3 vols. (Cambridge: Cambridge University Press, 1963), p.166. Also see Butterworth, pp. 213-14.

21. The original scriptures were *not* written with chapters and verses. The first known usage of chapters and verses together occurred in the thirteenth century by Stephen Langton for his own use as a teacher. (See Beryl Smalley, *The Study of the Bible in the Middle Ages* [Oxford: At the Clarendon Press, 1941], pp. 180-83.) Some scholars point out that these insertions can actually hinder a correct understanding of the scriptures because they give an artificial break to the message and encourage readers to take passages out of context. However, they continue to be used because they provide a convenient form of reference.

22. MacGregor, p. 160; Butterworth, pp. 215-16.

23. Clark, p. 32.

24. Ibid., p. 34.

25. Millicent J. Taylor, *Treasure of Free Men* (New York: Harper and Bros., 1953), p. 23; Butterworth, pp. 224, 312.

26. Butterworth, p. 21.

27. Ibid., p. 228. For elaboration see all of chapter 12.

28. Ibid., pp. 236-37.

29. Ibid., p. 237.

30. Ibid., p. 242.
31. Ibid., pp. 320-26.
32. MacGregor, p. 192; Butterworth, p. 240; H. G. G. Herklots, *How Our Bible Came to Us* (New York: Oxford University Press, 1954), p. 12.
33. Bruce, p. 107.
34. Ira Maurice Price, *The Ancestry of Our English Bible,* third revised edition by William A. Irwin and Allen P. Wikgren (New York: Harper and Row, 1956), pp. 275-76.
35. See Clark, especially notes (chapters) 26-34.
36. Clark, pp. 3-7, 60-61.
37. John Livingston Lowes as quoted in Butterworth, p. 5.
38. Bratton, pp. 263-64.
39. MacGregor, p. 192.

Notes to Chapter 8

1. United States Constitution, Amendment 1.
2. Millicent J. Taylor, *Treasure of Free Men* (New York: Harper and Brothers, 1953), p. 71.
3. Ibid., p. 72.
4. One specific influence of the Bible upon the pursuit of freedom can be found in words taken from Leviticus. These words, which originally proclaimed the Jubilee, or year of freedom, were inscribed on the Liberty Bell celebrating America's Declaration of Independence: "Proclaim Liberty Throughout All The Land Unto All The Inhabitants Thereof." (See Lev. 25:10.)
5. See 2 Nephi 3; Isaiah 11; Joseph Smith-History 1:33-41.
6. Eric M. North, ed., *The Book of a Thousand Tongues* (New York: Harper and Brothers, 1938), p. 13.
7. Ernest Christian Helmreich, *The German Churches under Hitler* (Detroit: Wayne State University Press, 1979), pp. 150, 234, 345, 466.
8. Carl Carmer, ed., *The War against God* (New York: Henry Holt and Co., 1943), p. 4.
9. Taylor, p. 38.
10. Ibid., p. 39.
11. Ibid., p. 73.
12. Luther A. Weigle, "English Versions Since 1611." *The West from the Reformation to the Present Day,* Vol. 3. of *Cambridge History of the Bible,* 3 vols. (Cambridge: Cambridge University Press, 1963), p. 385.
13. Parts of the Bible have actually been translated into 1600 of the world's 3000 languages or dialects; the entire Bible has been translated into approximately 200 of these. The Bible is now in the tongues *of over 97 percent* of the world's population; the remaining dialects are of small tribes or groups of people. Translative work still continues. See *The Book of a Thousand Tongues,* rev. and ed. Eugene A. Nida (London: United Bible Societies, 1972), p. viii. See also *Church News,* Nov. 28, 1981, p. 3.

14. Weigle, p. 389.
15. Taylor, p. 47.
16. North, p. 77.
17. Ibid., p. 79.

Notes to Chapter 9

1. Hugh W. Nibley, *Since Cumorah* (Salt Lake City, Utah: Deseret Book, 1967), p. 26.

2. *History of the Church* 1:132.

3. See Hugh W. Nibley, "To Open the Last Dispensation: Moses Chapter 1," in *Nibley on the Timely and the Timeless* (Provo, Utah: Religious Studies Center, Brigham Young University, 1978), pp. 1-20.

4. *Teachings of the Prophet Joseph Smith*, comp. Joseph Fielding Smith (Salt Lake City, Utah: Deseret Book, 1976), p. 327.

5. Robert J. Matthews, *"A Plainer Translation": Joseph Smith's Translation of the Bible, a History and Commentary* (Provo, Utah: Brigham Young University Press, 1975), p. 12.

6. "To William W. Phelps, July 31, 1832," in *The Personal Writings of Joseph Smith*, ed. Dean C. Jessee (Salt Lake City, Utah: Deseret Book, 1984), p. 248.

7. Robert J. Matthews, "The Bible and Its Role in the Restoration," *Ensign*, July 1979, p. 45.

8. Donald Q. Cannon and Lyndon W. Cook, eds., *Far West Record: Minutes of The Church of Jesus Christ of Latter-day Saints, 1830-1844* (Salt Lake City, Utah: Deseret Book, 1983), p. 23.

9. *History of the Church* 5:293.

10. Lavina Fielding Anderson, "Church Publishes First LDS Edition of the Bible," *Ensign*, October 1979, pp. 11-12.

11. Letter from Spencer W. Kimball, acting president of the Council of the Twelve, dated October 27, 1972, and sent to Dr. Ellis T. Rasmussen and Dr. Robert C. Patch.

12. For details of the work involved, see Anderson, pp. 12-14; Eleanor Knowles, "The Scriptures: A Personal Odyssey," in *A Woman's Choices: The Relief Society Legacy Lecture Series* (Salt Lake City, Utah: Deseret Book, 1984), pp. 151-57; and William James Mortimer, "The Coming Forth of the LDS Editions of Scripture," *Ensign*, August 1983, pp. 35-41.

13. "Appendix," in King James Version of the Holy Bible (Salt Lake City, Utah: The Church of Jesus Christ of Latter-day Saints, 1979), p. 802.

14. Edward J. Brandt, "The Development of the New LDS Bible," address given October 19, 1979.

15. See note 12.

16. See Anderson, pp. 14-15; Mortimer, p. 39.

17. Mortimer, p. 40.

18. Anderson, p. 15

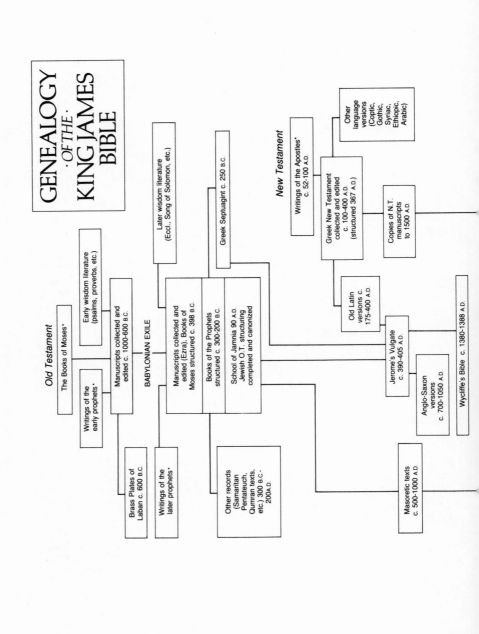

GENEALOGY
·OF THE·
KING JAMES BIBLE

Old Testament

The Books of Moses*

Early wisdom literature (psalms, proverbs, etc.)

Writings of the early prophets*

Manuscripts collected and edited c. 1000-600 B.C.

BABYLONIAN EXILE

Later wisdom literature (Eccl., Song of Solomon, etc.)

Manuscripts collected and edited (Ezra). Books of Moses structured c. 398 B.C.

Greek Septuagint c. 250 B.C.

Books of the Prophets structured c. 300-200 B.C.

School of Jamnia 90 A.D. Jewish O.T. structuring completed and canonized

Brass Plates of Laban c. 600 B.C.

Writings of the later prophets*

Other records (Samaritan Pentateuch, Qumran texts, etc.) 300 B.C.- 200 A.D.

New Testament

Writings of the Apostles* c. 52-100 A.D.

Other language versions (Coptic, Gothic, Syriac, Ethiopic, Arabic)

Greek New Testament collected and edited c. 100-400 A.D. (structured 367 A.D.)

Copies of N.T. manuscripts to 1500 A.D.

Old Latin versions c. 175-400 A.D.

Jerome's Vulgate c. 390-405 A.D.

Anglo-Saxon versions c. 700-1050 A.D.

Wycliffe's Bible c. 1380-1388 A.D.

Masoretic texts c. 500-1000 A.D.

PRINTING PRESS INVENTED: Latin Vulgate is published in 1456 (the Gutenberg Bible); hereafter, the scriptures are printed and made increasingly available to scholars and laymen alike.

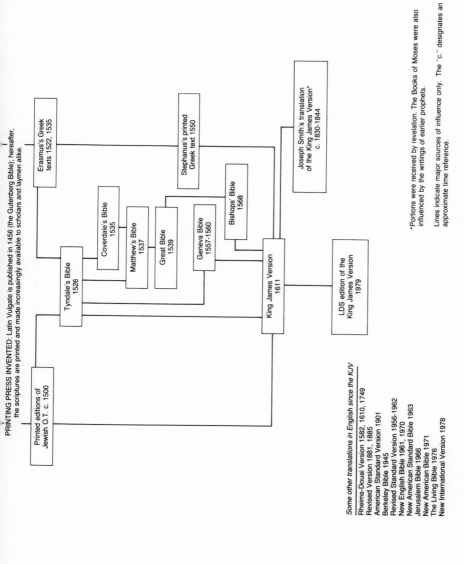

Printed editions of Jewish O.T. c. 1500

Erasmus's Greek texts 1522, 1535

Tyndale's Bible 1526

Coverdale's Bible 1535

Matthew's Bible 1537

Great Bible 1539

Geneva Bible 1557-1560

Bishops' Bible 1568

Stephanus's printed Greek text 1550

Joseph Smith's translation of the King James Version* c. 1830-1844

King James Version 1611

LDS edition of the King James Version 1979

*Portions were received by revelation. The Books of Moses were also influenced by the writings of earlier prophets.

Lines indicate major sources of influence only. The "c." designates an approximate time reference.

Some other translations in English since the KJV

Rheims-Douai Version 1582, 1610, 1749
Revised Version 1881, 1885
American Standard Version 1901
Berkeley Bible 1945
Revised Standard Version 1956-1962
New English Bible 1961, 1970
New American Standard Bible 1963
Jerusalem Bible 1966
New American Bible 1971
The Living Bible 1976
New International Version 1978

Index

Abraham, 4, 26, 101-3
Acts of the Apostles, 26
Adam, 2-3
Aelfric, 52
Aldhelm, 50
Alfred, King, 51-52
Allegories, Biblical events seen as, 39-40, 46
Alphabet, semitic, 3
Anderson, Richard L., 31
Anglo-Saxon, 50-52, 89
Animal skin for records, 13-14
Anthropomorphism, 17, 40
Antiochus, 19
Antwerp, 70, 73
Apocrypha, 42, 116-17
Apostles: writings of, 25-28, 30-31, 33-35; sufferings of, 32-33
Aramaic, 9, 17
Ashton, Marvin J., 106
Athanasius, 41-42
Authorship of books of Moses, 6-7

Bancroft, Richard, 83-84
Baruch, 10, 117
Bede, 49-51
Bethlehem, 44
Bible: importance, 1, 91-94, 111, 121; origins, 2-3; record-keeping, 4-5, 13-15; effect on myths, 5-6; writings of Moses, 6-7; books lost then found, 7-9; completion of Old Testament, 9-11; style and form, 15-17; translation into Greek, 17-19, 21; Old Testament during time of Christ, 19-21; Old Testament after time of Christ, 21-23; Gospels, 25-30; Christ's contributions to Gospels, 28-29; missing and corrupted records, 29-31, 101-3; letters, 30-31, 34-35; formation of New Testament, 31-33; Book of Revelation, 33-34; closing of Biblical record, 35; extensive use by early Christians, 37-39; problems with interpretation, 39-40; declining scriptural usage, 41, 46-47; canon of scripture decided, 41-42; Jerome and the Vulgate, 42-46; Christianity spread to Britain, 49-50; translation into Anglo-Saxon, 50-52; policy against translation, 52-53, 116-17; Waldensians, 53-55; Wycliffe translation, 55-61, 63; German translation, 62-63; invention of printing press, 63, 65; translations of Erasmus and Ximines, 66-67, 118; Tyndale translation, 67-74,

79-80; Coverdale translation,
74-78; Matthew Bible, 76-77; Great
Bible, 77-78; Geneva Bible, 78-79;
Bishops' Bible, 79; King James
sponsors translation, 81-83; King
James Version, 83-88; influences
on King James Version, 88-91;
revisions and impact of King
James Version, 91-92; Bible feeds
spirit of freedom, 93-94, 121;
influence of Bible on restoration,
94-96; fight against Bible, 96-97,
111; translation into non-
European languages, 97-99, 121;
restored portions of Bible, 101-3;
Joseph Smith Translation, 103-5;
LDS edition of King James
Version, 106-9; conclusion,
109-11; chart on Bible genealogy,
124-25
Biblical studies, early methods of,
39-40
Bishops' Bible, 79, 84-86, 89-90
Boards, writing, 13
Bois, John, 83
Book of Abraham, 4, 101-3
Book of Mormon, 1-2, 101-2, 106-8
Book of Moses, 2-4, 6-7, 102-3
Book of Revelation, 33-34
Brass plates, 1
Burmese Bible, 98-99
Butterworth, Charles, 90

Caedmon, 50
Cambridge University Press, 109
Canon of scripture, 21, 37-38, 42
Captivity, Babylonian, 8-10
Carthage, council of, 42
Catholic Church. See Christianity;
Inquisition; Popes
Chapters, scriptural division into, 120
Character, moral, impact of Bible on,.
96-97, 99
Chart on genealogy of Bible, 124-25
Chiasmus, 16
Christianity: use of scriptures by
first Christians, 20-21, 37-39;
early Christians embrace New
Word, 25; confusion over

doctrine, 31; persecutions of early
leaders, 32-33; canon of scripture,
37-38, 42; problems with
interpretation, 39-40; lessening
use of scriptures, 41, 46-47;
opposition to Jerome's translation,
44-45; acceptance of Vulgate,
45-46; Christianity spreads to
Britain, 49-51; Inquisition and
Waldensians, 53-55; early efforts
in England to translate Bible,
55-59; initial reactions to
English Bibles, 57-61; effect of
Renaissance, 65-67; opposition
to Tyndale translation, 68-73;
reaction over Coverdale's work
and the Matthew Bible, 74-78;
reception of Geneva and Bishops'
Bibles, 78-79; favorable climate
in England toward translation,
81-84, 87; effect of Bible on
man, 92-96
Civilization, flowering of, in
England, 51-52
Clark, J. Reuben, Jr., 91-92
Clay tablets, 13
Clement of Rome, 32
Clergy, scriptural knowledge among,
117. See also Christianity
Codex form for scriptures, 38
Coleman, Roger, 109
Cologne, 69
Computer, help of, in LDS editions,
108-9
Constantine, 41
Constantinople, fall of, 65-66
Conversion through Septuagint, 20
Copying of scriptures. See Records,
Scriptures, copies of
Copyists, 47. See also Scribes, work of
Cost of Bible, 60
Council of Jamnia, 21
Coverdale, Miles: assists Tyndale
in translation, 72; finishes
Tyndale's translation, 74-76;
works on Great Bible, 76-78; flees
to Geneva, 78-79
Coverdale Bible, 74-75, 84-86, 89
Cranmer, Archbishop, 76, 78

Cromwell, 74-78
Cross-referencing scriptures, 106-8

Damasus, Pope, 43-44
Dead Sea Scrolls, 22, 28
Destruction of scriptures, 38-39, 60,
    70-72, 78, 116-17
Dispensation, ending of, 35
Doctrine, confusion over, 31
Doctrine and Covenants, 95, 106-8
Douai versions, 84

Edward, King, 78
Egbert, Bishop, 51
Elizabeth, Queen, 79
England: Christianity spreads to,
    49-51; King Alfred's rule over,
    51-52; Wycliffe's efforts in, to
    improve knowledge of scriptures,
    55-58; Purvey's efforts in, to
    translate, 57, 59-60; reaction in,
    over Tyndale translation, 70-73;
    official sanction in, for
    translations, 74-79; King James
    translation made in, 81-84, 87-89
English. See England; Translation
Enoch, 4
Erasmus, 66-68, 118
Eusebius, 38
Ezra, 8-9

Fausset, A. R., 28
Footnotes in LDS editions, 106-8
Form in Old Testament, 15-17
France, 77
Freedom, spirit of, 93-94, 121
French, 53-54
Friends of God, 62
Fyans, J. Thomas, 106

Genealogy of King James Bible,
    124-25
"Generations of," meaning of, 4
Geneva Bible, 78-79
German translation, 61-63, 68
Germany, 61-63, 68-69, 71-72
Gilby paraphrase of scripture, 86
Gileadi, Avraham, 16
God, index entries for, 108

Gospel, restoration of, 94-96
Gospels: the four Gospels, 25,
    28-29; Matthew, 25-26; Mark,
    26, 30; Luke, 26; John, 26-27;
    Christ's contribution to Gospels,
    28-29; lost books, 29-30;
    differences between Gospels and
    letters, 30-31
Great Bible, 77-79, 85, 89
Greek, 18, 66, 88-89, 107-8. See also
    Septuagint
Greene, John Richard, 96
Gregory VII, Pope, 52-53
Gutenberg, Johann, 65

Hamburg, 68-69, 71-72
Harrison, R. K., 4
Hebrew, 9, 21-22, 44-45, 88-89. See
    also Old Testament
Hebrews. See Jews
Henry VIII, King, 74-78
Hereford, Nicholas de, 57-58
Hexapla, 40
Historical books, 9
Hitler, Adolf, 96-97
Holland, 70-71, 73
Hope of Israel's record, 6

Impact of Bible: on language, 92;
    on religion, 93; on spirit of
    freedom, 93-94; on restoration
    of gospel, 94-96; on moral
    character, 96-97, 99
Imprisonment for translation, 58, 60,
    73, 99
Index to Triple Combination, 107-8
Inquisition, 53-55, 59-62, 116-17
Interpretation of scriptures, 39-40
Irenaeus, 38
Isaiah, 10, 16
Israel, history of, 2-6, 8-9

James, King, 81-83, 87
Jehoiakim, King, 10
Jeremiah, 10-11, 16
Jerome: work of, 42-45; translation
    by, of Bible, 45-47, 57

Jesus Christ: similitudes of, 16; relation of, and Old Testament, 19-21, 39; Gospels testify of, 25-30; during forty days after his resurrection, 30; New Testament focuses on, 31-32; John sees resurrected, 34; effect of Bible message of, 96; baptism of, 107-8; Topical Guide entries for, 108

Jews, 2-3, 21-23, 35. See also Old

John, writings of, 26-27, 33-34

Joseph Smith Translation, 95, 103-5, 107-8

Josephus, 18

Judson, Adoniram, 98-99

King James Version: sponsoring by king, 81-83; method of translation, 83-87; completion, 87-88; influences on translation, 88-91; attempts at revision, 91-92; impact on world, 92; Joseph Smith Translation, 95, 102-5; different editions, 106; Latter-day Saint edition, 106-9; chart on genealogy, 124-25

Language, 15-17, 92, 97-98, See also Greek; Hebrew; Latin; Translation

Latin, 43-46, 50, 61, 65-66, 88-89. See also Translation

Latter-day Saint edition of King James Version, 106-9

Law of Moses, 7-9

Leather for records, 13-14

Lehi, 1

Letters of New Testament, 30-31, 33-34

Liberty Bell, 121

Light from scriptures, 52, 63, 93, 101, 109-11

Lollards, 56

Lost books, 7-9, 11, 29-30, 102

Luke, 26

Luther, Martin, 68-69

Mark, 26

Masoretes, 21-22

Matthew, 25-26

Matthew Bible, 75-77

Matthews, Robert J., 103-5

McConkie, Bruce R., 6, 34-35, 106

Meanings, double, use of, 16

Middle Ages, 49

Middle English, 56-59

Missionary work in England, 49-50

Monmouth (merchant), 68

Monotype, 109

Monson, Thomas S., 106

Morality, impact of Bible on, 96-97, 99

More, Thomas, 70-71, 74

Moses, 2-4, 6-7, 16, 102-3

Myths based on Bible, 5-6

New Testament: individual Gospels, 25-27; Gospels considered collectively, 28-30; letters, 30-31, 33-34; story behind New Testament, 31-33; Paul, 32-33; Book of Revelation, 33-34; gift of Bible, 35; authoritative canon decided, 37-38, 42; translations into classical languages, 44, 66; Tyndale translates and prints New Testament, 68-72. See also Translation

Nibley, Hugh, 3, 7-8, 42, 102-3

"Nought," 118

Old Testament: record of Jews, 2-3; record-keeping, 4-5, 9-11, 13-14; myths based on Old Testament, 5-6; writings of Moses, 6-7; the Law—lost and found, 7-9; scribes, 14-15; style and form, 15-17; challenges of translation, 17-19; Old Testament during time of Christ, 19-21; Old Testament after time of Christ, 21-23; accepted canon, 42; translation into Latin, 44-45; Wycliffe translation interrupted, 57-58; Tyndale translates and prints Pentateuch, 71-72. See also Septuagint; Translation

Order of books in Old Testament, 11

Origen, 39-40

Origin of bible, 2-3

Packer, Boyd K., 106
Packington (merchant), 70-71
Papias, 25-26
Papyrus, 13
Patriarchs keep records, 4
Paul, 26, 32-33
Pearl of Great Price: Book of Moses, 2-4, 6-7, 102-3; Book of Abraham, 4, 101-3; references to records, 4-5; revelations, 95, 102; Triple Combination 106-8
Pentateuch, 6-7, 9, 71-72
Persecution: of early Christians, 32-33; aimed at destroying scriptures, 38-39, 60, 70-72, 78, 116-17; of Wycliffe, 56-57; over Wycliffe Bible, 57-61; of William Tyndale, 68-73; anti-Protestant, in England, 78; modern, over Bible, 96-97, 111
Peter, 26, 32
Phelps, William W., 104
Poetry, Hebrew, 15
Popes: Pope Damasus, 43-44; Pope Gregory VII, 52-53, 61; papal schism, 55-56
Prayer Book, 85
Preservation of records, 13-15, 19
Printing press, 63, 65, 68-72, 109, 125
Prison. See Imprisonment for translation
Prophets, record-keeping of, 5
Psalms, 41, 51, 53, 85-86
Ptolemy, King, 18
Puritans, 81-94
Purvey, John, 57-60

Record of Jews, 2-3
Records, 2-6, 13-17, 19. See also Scriptures, copies of
Religion, impact of Bible on, 93-94
"Religion of the Book," 8, 21
Renaissance, effect of, on scriptures, 65-67
Restoration of gospel, 94-96, 101-5
Revelation, Book of, 33-34
Revelation sparked by Joseph Smith Translation, 95, 103-5
Revisions of King James Bible, 91,103

Reynolds, John, 81-83
Rheims-Douai Version, 84, 90
Rogers, John, 76, 78

Sanchez, Margaret Tuttle, 85-86
Scholarship, Biblical, to produce translations. See Translation
Scribes, work of, 7, 14-15
Scriptures. See Bible; Book of Mormon; Doctrine and Covenants; Pearl of Great Price
Scriptures, copies of: discovering ancient, 8-9, 22, 28, 42, 99; making and preserving, 14, 18-19, 21-22, 41, 46-47, 56; cost of, 60; printing of English Bibles, 69-72, 74-79, 87-88, 109, 125. See also Records
Scrolls, 13-14, 22, 37-38
Seldon, John, 85
Septuagint, 11, 18, 20-21, 43-44
Sermon on the Mount, 80, 90-91
Similitudes in scriptures, 16-17
Smith, Joseph, 94-95, 102-5
Smith, Joseph Fielding, 106
Smith, Miles, 88
Spain, 116-17
Spanish, 62
Style in Old Testament, 6-7, 15-17
Support, lack of, for Joseph Smith, 105

Tabernacle, Israelite, 45
Targums, 17
Theodore of Tarsus, 49-50
Topical Guide, 107-8
Translation: oral translation, 17; Septuagint, 18, 20-21; new Greek translation, 21; the Vulgate, 43-46; Anglo-Saxon translations, 50-52; policy against translations, 52-53, 116-17; Waldensians, 53-55; Wycliffe translation, 55-60, 63, 89-91, 118; translation in Germany, 61-63; New Testament translations into classical languages, 66; Tyndale translation, 68-73, 79-80, 84, 89-90; Coverdale Bible, 74-76, 84-86,

89-90; Matthew Bible, 75-77; Great
Bible, 77-79, 85, 90; Geneva Bible,
78-79, 82, 84-86, 89-91; Bishops'
Bible, 79, 84-86, 89-91; King James
Version commissioned, 81-83;
method of translation of King
James Version, 83-87; completion
of King James Version, 87-88;
influences on King James Version,
88-91; modern translations, 91-92,
97-98, 121; Joseph Smith
Translation, 95, 103-5, 107-8;
Zanaki language translation, 98;
Burmese translation, 98-99
Translators of King James Version:
    choice of, 82-83; work of, 84-87,
    90
"Translators to the Readers," 88
Triple Combination, 106-8
Truth in Bible, 111
Tudor, Mary, 78-79
Tunstal, 68, 70-71
Tyndale, William: background of,
    67-68; translates and prints New
    Testament, 68-72; translates and
    prints Pentateuch, 71-72; final
    days of, 73, 75
Tyndale translation, 68-72, 79-80, 84,
    89-90. See also Coverdale Bible;
    Matthew Bible
Typeface, new, 109

Vellum, 41, 47
Verses, divisions into, 120
Vilvorde Castle, 73
Vocabulary, ecclesiastical, 46
Vulgate, 43-46, 57. See also
    Translation

Waldensians, 53-55, 61-62
Waldo, 53
Washington, George, 94
Wilson, Woodrow, 94
Wittenberg, 68
Worms, 69
Worship: scriptures central to, 37-38;
    in Middle Ages, 50, 61
Writing boards, 13
"Writings," 11
Wycliffe, John, 55-58
Wycliffe translation: first version,
    55-58; second version, 58-59; fate,
    59-60; sample, 63; influence on
    King James Version, 89;
    translation of "nought," 118

Ximines, 66-67

Young, Brigham, 105

Zanaki language, 98